LET'S GET
TROPICAL

Penguin
Random
House

Editors Laura Bithell, Anna Cheifetz
Designer Vanessa Hamilton
Jacket Designer Steve Marsden
Managing Editor Dawn Henderson
Art Director Maxine Pedliham
Publishing Director Mary-Clare Jerram
Producer, Pre-production
Heather Blagden
Producer Stephanie McConnell
Photography Ruth Jenkinson
Special Sales Creative
Project Manager Alison Donovan

First published in Great Britain in
2019 by Dorling Kindersley Limited
80 Strand, London WC2R 0RL

Copyright © 2019
Dorling Kindersley Limited
A Penguin Random House Company

2 4 6 8 10 9 7 5 3 1

001 – 314161 – May/2019

A CIP catalogue record for this book
is available from the British Library.

ISBN 978-0-2413-7895-3

Printed and bound in China

All images © Dorling Kindersley Limited

A WORLD OF IDEAS:
SEE ALL THERE IS TO KNOW

www.dk.com

CONTENTS

Author's note 4

A TASTE OF THE TROPICS 6

Tropical cocktail history 8
How is rum made? 12
Which rum is which? 14
Other tropical spirits & liqueurs 16
Tools & equipment 18
Get further equipped 20
Glass gallery 22
Shake it up 26
Mix like a pro 28
Make it at home 30
Make your own mix 34
Classic garnishes 36
Creative garnishes 38
Sharing is caring 40
Top 10 quick wins 42

CLASSIC COCKTAILS & TWISTS 44

Caipirinha 46
Queen's Park Swizzle 50
Daiquiri 52
Rum Punch 56
Piña Colada 60
Pornstar Martini 64
Singapore Sling 66
Blue Hawaii 70
Mai Tai 72

Fog Cutter 76
Jungle Bird 80
Margarita 82
Tequila Sunrise 86
Pearl Diver 90
Blue Lagoon 94
Hurricane 96
Mojito 100
Nui Nui 104
Miami Vice 106
Sex on the Beach 110
Rum Runner 114

MODERN TROPICAL COCKTAILS 116

Taki Fugu 118
Tiki Daddy G 120
Beach Whacker 122
Tropical Apple Toffee 124
Tiki Tiki Bang Bang 126
Laki Lambo 128
Golden Sand 130
English Tea-Ki Garden 132
Makana 134
Lanai Punch 136
Wiki Tiki 138
Angels' Share 140

Index and acknowledgments 142

AUTHOR'S note

I started writing this book during the busiest time of my life. I had just opened my bar, Laki Kane, and I was flying all over the world giving presentations on tropical drinks. With only one week to spare during my holiday with the family, this book began life as ideas and notes written lying on the beach in the sun, listening to the crashing waves, and enjoying the soft sea breeze. The setting couldn't have been more fitting.

Getting to where I am today has been a long time in the making. I graduated in banking and insurance, but it was quickly apparent that working in an office wasn't for me. I was instead drawn to hospitality – I needed to be around people, to entertain and spread happiness. So, in my early 20s, I travelled to London to learn about the drinks industry. Douglas Ankrah introduced me to modern tropical cocktails at the legendary Lab and Townhouse bars, Richard Wood taught me all about rum at La Floridita, and Papa Jules introduced me to the tiki and tropical lifestyle when I joined the Mahiki team. I was hooked – I fell for the beautiful nature, the exotic flavours, but most of all the tropical culture of harmonious living and passing love and positive energy. Our industry is all about making people happy, and that makes me happy. It wasn't long before I was promoted to Global Creative Manager for Mahiki.

All of these years of experience were leading to the opening of my own London bar, Laki Kane. The words together refer to the "lucky sugar cane" that makes the best rum; translate them separately, and "laki" means "lucky" and "kane" means "human". We wanted to make everyone entering the bar feel lucky and happy. Don the

mixology and presentation techniques, and we even distil our own unique Spice Dry Rum on site – I think Don the Beachcomber would be proud!

The cocktails in this book are an accumulation of everything I've learned from my travels and my work. From the first Caribbean rum punches to a selection of original modern drinks (and everything in between!), they are a real testament to tropical cocktail history and evolution.

You might want to read up on the stories behind the cocktails, or you might want to skip all of that and get straight to the Margaritas, it's up to you! You may even want to take a leaf out of my and Don the Beachcomber's book and come up with your own original mix. This book is all about sharing the pleasure that comes with a cocktail, so take from it what appeals to you the most. Let's get tropical!

Beachcomber's tiki cocktail concept was so creative that bars and bartenders are still trying to recreate and enhance his drinks almost 100 years later. We wanted our bar to be as innovative, and to start a new era of tropical drinks. Laki Kane doesn't just take its inspiration from tiki, it is an escape to every tropical destination you've ever wanted to visit. We use rare exotic fruits, homemade syrups using natural sugars, cutting-edge

Tropical cocktails are all about using delicious ingredients from **tropical destinations**. They make use of the **fresh fruits** and **exotic spices**, and immediately conjure up an image of a place. So **where do they come from**, **what are they made of**, and how can you create your own **island escape** at home?

A TASTE OF THE TROPICS

Tropical cocktail HISTORY

From Mayan cocoa to Kava root concoctions on the Pacific islands, tropical drinks certainly existed in the Pre-Columbian era. However, it's only in the last few centuries that the boozy cocktails we know and love today began to emerge.

PACKING A PUNCH

All recognizable tropical cocktails originate from the rum punch. The first written record of the word "punch" to describe an alcoholic drink dates back to 1632, but people were most likely making punch drinks long before this. The word comes from the Hindu for "five", representing the different constituents in a punch drink – sour, sweet, strong, weak, and spice. This is the template for almost every tropical cocktail.

In the 16th century, sugar was more expensive than gold. When Europeans realized that the Caribbean and South America had the perfect climate for growing sugar cane, they began investing in big plantations. Soon it was discovered that alcohol (rum) could be made cheaply from molasses, a by-product of the sugar industry. By the end of the 17th century, rum had become the drink of the Caribbean islands, the British Navy, and pirates, and was being exported in large quantities to Europe. It worked perfectly with sugar, citrus, and spices and rum punch became the drink of choice in England and the colonies.

NAVY RUM

In the 17th century, rum became the official spirit of the British Navy and a ration of rum was given to every British sailor. "Navy strength" meant an alcohol content above 57%. To keep discipline and promote health, the rum was watered down and mixed with energising sugar and vitamin-packed citrus to make what became known as "Grog" (named after the Admiral who invented it). This was one of the earliest tropical cocktails.

THE PROS OF PROHIBITION

This sober period of history actually had a positive effect on tropical cocktail evolution. With dodgy booze being produced illegally in North America, many people were more trusting of alcohol sourced from the Caribbean and nearby Mexico.

THE CARIBBEAN BOOM

By the 1920s, the sugar plantations were focused on producing high-quality rum. Americans and Europeans were already fond of rum punches, and nothing tasted better with rum than the amazing fresh tropical fruits and unique spices available on the islands. Big hotels popped up and began to develop delicious signature drinks, and soon the tourist industry was booming.

CUBAN COCKTAIL CULTURE

Cuba had already made an impact on the cocktail scene in the late 1800s with the invention of a more palatable, light-style rum. During Prohibition, many bartenders moved to Cuba and established great cocktail bars – and classic cocktails, such as the Daiquiri and the Mojito.

MEXICAN MARGARITAS

Mexico was a another popular Prohibition-era escape. Bourbon and Cognac weren't available, so people started drinking tequila instead. The most famous outcome was Mexico's first tropical cocktail, the Margarita.

COCKTAIL HISTORY CONTINUED ▶

AROUND THE WORLD

The popularity of tropical flavours encouraged the innovation of iconic cocktails in bars and hotels all over the world. The Raffles Hotel in Singapore produced the Singapore Sling, while the Jungle Bird was invented at the Kuala Lumpur Hilton. North America was also the source of many famous tropical cocktails.

TIKI TRAVELS

One of the most significant events in the history of tropical cocktails was the invention of the tiki bar. The concept was devised by Ernest Raymond Beaumont Gantt – better known as Don the Beachcomber. During the Prohibition era in the 1920s, he travelled to the Caribbean in search of good rum to bring back to alcohol-deprived Americans. He enjoyed the tropical lifestyle of the Caribbean and extended his travels to the South Pacific, where he fell in love with the beautiful islands and the Aloha culture and spirit. He returned to America with an array of souvenirs and decorations from his trip, as well as a vast knowledge of rum and rum punches.

In 1933, Gantt opened the first tiki bar in Hollywood called Don's Beachcomber, later renamed Don the Beachcomber. The drinks he created were incredibly innovative, featuring homemade fresh ingredients, fantastic rum blends, theatrical presentation, and cheeky names. No one had seen or tasted anything like them, and they were quickly a hit! Soon, rivals such as Trader Vic (Victor Jules Bergeron Jr.), inventor of the iconic Mai Tai, began to set up their own bars serving tiki drinks. By the 1950s and '60s, tiki had become so popular that every big city in America had at least one tiki bar.

DISCO DRINKS

By the 1970s and '80s, everyone wanted a piece of the tiki pie, and many big, busy tiki bars opened up. However, it was impossible to mass-produce the carefully crafted, homemade cocktails of Don the Beachcomber and Trader Vic, so bars started cheating when making the drinks, or inventing entirely new drinks using fewer, simpler ingredients. Disco versions of the classics began to appear and some of the most recognizable tropical drinks, such as the Blue Lagoon and Sex on the Beach, were invented. This period marked a step forward in the evolution of cocktail ingredients, as many commercial syrups and liqueurs started to appear, but these took some of the craft out of the cocktail.

TROPICAL TODAY

Tropical drinks and bars are making a big return. In 2006, Mahiki opened in London bringing tiki into the 21st century with new tropical drinks, and inspiring great modern American tiki bars like Smuggler's Cove, Three Dots and a Dash, and Latitude 29. Now bars such as London's Laki Kane are taking the best elements of traditional tropical cocktails and tiki culture and using them to create innovative new cocktail menus. In a world where almost any tropical ingredient is available in the local supermarket, the key is to capture the sense of exoticism evoked by the original tiki cocktails. This is why innovative bartenders are turning to lesser-known ingredients. Have you ever tried a drink with sweet jackfruit, sapodilla, rambutan, star fruit, or dragon fruit?

How is RUM MADE?

Rum is the most versatile spirit in the world. Originating as a way of recycling leftovers from the sugar industry, it has less rigid rules than other spirits – it can be made using a range of sugar cane products and methods of distillation and ageing, resulting in a variety of styles.

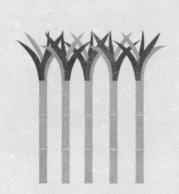

THE BASE INGREDIENT

All spirits start with a raw base ingredient. For a spirit to be labelled "rum", this has to be a sugar cane product. The sugar cane is milled to extract sugar cane juice. The juice is then processed to make molasses and sugar. The majority of rums are made from molasses, but agricole rum is made from the raw sugar cane juice.

FERMENTATION

Either yeast inherent in the sugar cane product is allowed to ferment naturally, or yeast is added artificially and fermentation controlled in vats. The yeast breaks down the molasses or sugar cane juice and converts it to a base alcohol called the "wash". Depending on the style of rum, this can take a few days to several weeks.

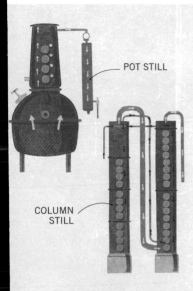

POT STILL

COLUMN
STILL

Did you know?
The portion of
rum that is lost to
distillation is called
the "Angels'
Share".

DISTILLATION

This process separates the alcohol from
the water in the wash through boiling
and evaporation. The alcohol evaporates
first and is then condensed back into
liquid. Alcohol carries lots of flavours, so
the distiller must choose which flavours
to keep during distillation. The
traditional pot still uses simple single
distillation to create a strong, crude
spirit. Although labour intensive and
expensive, this method distils to a lower
percentage of alcohol and keeps more
of the flavours to create a "heavy" style
rum. The modern column still uses
continuous distillation to control the
separation of the vapours, it distils to
a much higher percentage of alcohol,
with fewer flavour components, and
creates a "light" style rum.

AGEING

This is what gives rum its colour. The
longer the rum is aged, the more it will
pick up the colour of the barrel, and the
darker it will become. Whilst ageing will
significantly change the flavour and
aroma of the rum, a column-distilled aged
rum will taste noticeably different to a
pot-distilled aged rum.

Which rum IS WHICH?

Rum is often simply grouped into white, gold, aged, and dark varieties. However, there are other things to consider when choosing your rum – the character of the rum is defined by the base ingredient, the distillation process, ageing, and any added ingredients.

SPICED & FLAVOURED RUMS

Spiced rums are made by macerating spices in the rum, filtrating them, then adding sugar. They are good for adding extra flavour to cocktails. Flavoured rums often have added sugar and a lower alcohol content, technically making them liqueurs. There are many flavoured rums, but the most popular is coconut rum.

LIGHT (SPANISH STYLE)

The ex-Spanish colonies, such as Cuba, Puerto Rico, the Dominican Republic, and Nicaragua, make light rum (or "ron") using a column still. The white rums are particularly light in flavour and perfect for Daiquiris and Mojitos, the gold rums have more character and are an excellent choice for more complex cocktails. The premium rums are often aged for a long time and have amazingly delicate characteristics.

WHITE

Bacardi Carta Blanca
(Puerto Rico)
Don Q Cristal *(Puerto Rico)*
Havana Anejo Blanco
(Cuba)
Flor de Caña 4
(Nicaragua)
Barcelo Gran Platinum
(Dominican Republic)

GOLDEN AGED

Bacardi Gold
(Puerto Rico)
Don Q Gold
(Puerto Rico)
Havana Anejo 3
(Cuba)
Brugal Anejo
(Dominican Republic)

PREMIUM AGED

Don Q Grand Anejo
(Puerto Rico)
Havana 15
(Cuba)
Brugal 1888
(Dominican Republic)
Flor De Caña 18
(Nicaragua)

HEAVY (BRITISH STYLE)

The ex-British colonies Jamaica, Barbados, St Lucia, and Guyana make heavier style rums. The rich flavours come from a longer fermentation process and the use of the traditional pot still. Rums made only with a pot still, known as Pure Single Rum, are heaviest and are most popular in Jamaica. Elsewhere, the most popular heavy rums are a blend of pot and column still rums, known as Single Blended Rum.

WHITE

El Dorado 3 (Guyana)
Doorly's 3 (Barbados)
Chairman's Reserve White (Guyana)
Rum-Bar Silver (Jamaica Pure Single Rum)

GOLDEN AGED

Mount Gay Eclipse (Barbados)
Chairman's Reserve (St Lucia)
El Dorado 5 (Guyana)
Appleton Estate Signature (Jamaica)
Rum-Bar Gold (Jamaica Pure Single Rum)

PREMIUM AGED

Mount Gay XO (Barbados)
Appleton Estate Rare Blend (Jamaica)
El Dorado 12 (Guyana)
Worthy Park Single Estate (Jamaica Pure Single Rum)

AGRICOLE

The ex-French colonies of Martinique, Guadeloupe, and Mauritius make their rum (or "rhum") from raw sugar cane juice rather than molasses. The notes are fruitier, grassier, and often a little earthy, herbal, and vegetal. The white rums are perfect for light cocktails and the gold rums work well with aged molasses rum in tropical drinks.

BRANDS

Trois Rivières (Martinique), **Clément** (Martinique), **Neisson** (Martinique), **St Aubin** (Mauritius), **Damoiseau** (Guadeloupe)

DARK

You'll often see dark, inexpensive rums in the shops. If these are labelled "dark" rather than "aged", the colour has nothing to do with ageing in barrels. The colour instead comes from the caramel added to the rum before it is bottled. These rums are rarely consumed neat, but they taste good in cocktails.

BRANDS

Lamb's Navy Rum (Caribbean blend), **Captain Morgan Original** (Caribbean), **Gosling's Black Seal** (Bermuda), **Myer's Original Dark** (Jamaica)

Other TROPICAL SPIRITS & LIQUEURS

It doesn't stop with rum – there are plenty of other delicious tropical liqueurs and spirits made from ingredients grown in, or originating from, tropical destinations. They all have distinctly different flavours depending on the base ingredient and where and how they're made. Below are the ones you'll see popping up in recipes throughout this book.

TEQUILA

To be classified as tequila, the spirit has to be made from the blue agave plant, and produced in Mexico in the region of Tequila. As with rum, tequila can processed with or without ageing. The lighter styles are fresher and fruitier than the darker styles, which will have picked up vanilla, caramel, and oak notes from ageing in barrels. There is less variety across tequila styles, so you can generally interchange them in your cocktails without upsetting the balance of flavours.

STYLES

Blanco (white) Rested for up to 3 months in glass or steel rather than aged in wood. The final product is clear.

Reposado (rested) Aged for up to 12 months in oak; this style is gold in colour.

Añejo (aged) Aged for up to 3 years in oak; this style is darker in colour.

CURAÇAO

This is an orange-flavoured liqueur made using the bitter Laraha orange – a variety grown on the island of Curaçao in the Caribbean. For hundreds of years, it has been used to make orange Curaçao (orange in colour) and Triple Sec (clear in colour). Both are sweet and orangey, although orange Curaçao is slightly more bitter. Blue Curacao is simply a blue-coloured version of the same drink. The slightly drier French liqueur, Cointreau, is mostly made using these oranges too. Curaçao and Triple Sec are normally under 40% alcohol, whereas Cointreau is stronger at 40% alcohol.

PISCO

This Chilean or Peruvian spirit is similar to brandy, although it is sweeter, fruitier, and more aromatic. Chilean Pisco is lighter and sweeter because it is distilled a few times and uses aromatic grapes such as Muscat. Peruvian Pisco is heavier because it is only distilled once and water is not added after distillation. Most varieties are unaged and clear.

CACHAÇA

Cachaça is a Brazilian sugar cane juice spirit that predates rum. It is distilled to a lower percentage of alcohol, so more of the sugar cane flavours are retained. It is usually unaged, although some aged Cachaças are gaining popularity. These have a unique flavour, as they are aged in special barrels made from Brazilian oak. Cachaça has a similar flavour to agricole rum – it is fruity, earthy, grassy, a little herbal, and very fresh.

MEZCAL

A lesser-known agave spirit, most mezcals are made in Wahaca, Mexico, in small, local distilleries. It has fewer production rules than tequila, and is made using many different types of agave. The most obvious difference to tequila is the smoky flavour, achieved by smoking the agave in big ground pits. It is rarely aged, so is usually clear in colour; but the flavour can vary depending on the agave variety.

TOOLS & EQUIPMENT

A basic cocktail set is essential for making and shaking drinks. Luckily, the equipment is easy to find and fairly inexpensive. You can get a good set online, in specialist bar shops, or sometimes even in your local supermarket.

1. THREE-PIECE SHAKER

The most common and traditional shaker, it is also the easiest to find. The bottom piece is the base, the middle piece is the strainer, and the top piece is the cup (lid).

2. BOSTON SHAKER

The shaker favoured by many bartenders. The bottom half (Boston glass) is where the ingredients are mixed. Clear glasses are best as you can see the colour of the drink. The top half (Boston tin), fits tightly on top of the glass.

3. STRAINER

The Hawthorne strainer has a coiled spring that fits tightly on top of the Boston glass for straining after shaking. The fine strainer is an extra strainer that can be used to ensure tiny pieces of ingredients and ice don't make it into the serving glass.

4. BAR JIGGER

This is your key measuring tool. There are many types, but a double jigger with measures inside is great for beginners. One side is 50ml ($1^2/_3$fl oz) and the other is 25ml ($^4/_5$fl oz).

5. BAR SPOON

A very handy tool, the bar spoon can be used to measure, stir, and swizzle drinks. The standard bar spoon is 5ml ($^1/_6$fl oz), although some can be 2.5ml ($^1/_{12}$fl oz), so it's best to check. Flat-bottomed spoons can also be used to muddle and churn.

BLENDER

You're going to need a blender to make a lot of the classic tropical drinks in this book. No need to buy anything specialist, your regular kitchen blender will do!

TOOLS & EQUIPMENT CONTINUED ▶

Get further EQUIPPED

These are extra, non-essential tools, but they will certainly aid your drink-making and help you impress your guests. With the popularity of home bars on the rise, even the most specialist equipment is getting easier to find. The best place to start is online bar shops.

1. CITRUS SQUEEZER

For squeezing fresh juice out of a lemon or lime just before you make a drink. It's an efficient way to extract maximum juice with minimum fuss.

2. MUDDLER

Used to squish or bruise ingredients, such as fresh fruits, vegetables, herbs, and spices, to extract flavour. If the recipe calls for "muddling", grab this tool.

3. PINEAPPLE CORER

This tool makes cutting up a pineapple so much easier and eliminates waste. You can use it to hollow out a big pineapple "glass", or to slice the flesh into neat rings to go inside a drink. You can even make use of the core to create round "coin" garnishes.

4. BAR SCOOP

A handy tool for shovelling ice. They come in lots of different sizes – a 24oz stainless steel scoop is a great choice, as it is big enough to use but feels comfortable to hold.

5. MELON BALLER

Not just for melons – use this tool to make perfect fruit ball garnishes out of many fruits including watermelon, papaya, pineapple, and banana.

6. BAR KNIFE

A bar knife (or any other small, very sharp knife) will really make a difference. It will help you precisely cut the part of the fruit you want – whether that's the juicy flesh or a piece of peel to make the perfect decoration.

7. ZESTER & PEELER

These are both primarily used to make garnishes out of citrus peel. The zester is perfect for making fine sprinklings of aromatic zest, and the peeler can be angled to cut different thicknesses of peel for beautiful twists

8. TONGS

Ideally, you should own a pair of tongs for hygiene, especially if you're making drinks for other people. Use them to pick up any solid ingredients, such as pieces of fruit and ice.

9. DUSTER

This handy tool allows you to cover your drink with an even, fine layer of sugar or spice to add visual appeal, flavour, and aroma.

10. NUTMEG GRATER

Although this is designed for nutmeg, you can use it for other ingredients. This great little grater also doubles up as a container for storing spices in when you're not using it.

GLASS *gallery*

Tropical cocktails brought variety and flair to the traditional range of glassware. Although most cocktails are associated with a specific glass, you can get creative with your choices as long as the liquid volume is roughly the same.

1. HURRICANE GLASS

Made famous by the Hurricane cocktail, this glass is designed to look like a hurricane lantern. It is typically used for long tropical cocktails, drinks served with crushed ice, and blended cocktails.

2. POCO GRANDE

Also known as the Piña Colada glass, it is similar to the hurricane but slightly shorter and fatter. It is usually used for blended drinks, but it can also be used for long drinks with crushed ice.

3. SLING GLASS

This glass is used for more classic tropical cocktails. Usually, these cocktails are shaken with ice, and they are often topped with fizz. The sling glass is very rarely used for blended drinks or for drinks with crushed ice.

4. HIGHBALL GLASS

Although this is not considered a tropical glass style, it is great for tropical swizzles, and is the preferred glass for some of the best tropical classics, including the Mojito and the Queen's Park Swizzle. Engraved tropical highballs are very popular at the moment.

5. ROCKS GLASS

Traditionally used for neat drinks on ice, the rocks glass is now a popular cocktail glass. It is attractive, elegant, and comes in many different shapes and designs.

6. BRANDY BALLOON

Also known as a "snifter", this glass is traditionally used for serving aged Cognacs or expensive spirits with amazing aromas. Its size and elegance makes it a great choice for tiki and tropical cocktails.

GLASS GALLERY CONTINUED

7. MARTINI & COUPE GLASSES

These are the ultimate elegant cocktail glasses. They are mainly used for short, shaken cocktails served without ice. The most famous tropical drink served in a coupe glass is the Daiquiri.

8. MARGARITA GLASS

This glass was invented specifically for the Margarita cocktail. However, it is also a great choice for any tropical drink with a tequila or mezcal base.

9. CHAMPAGNE FLUTE

Often used for tropical-style cocktails with sparkling wine or sophisticated cocktails without ice.

10. PEARL DIVER GLASS

Although this glass was designed specifically for the Pearl Diver cocktail, it is a great choice for any flash-blended tropical cocktail.

11. TIKI GLASSES & MUGS

Tiki mugs were created alongside the first tiki drinks as works of art to represent tiki culture and give the cocktail a theatrical appearance. Now, every tiki bar is trying to create the best tiki mug design. They are also a practical way to disguise a drink that may not look as good as it tastes! If the colour of your drink is worth showing off, clear tiki glasses are now fairly easy to get hold of.

HOLLOWED FRUITS

When hollowed, big fruits such as pineapples, melons, and grapefruits make great "glasses". Try making one with a pineapple corer.

1. Cut off the top of the fruit.

2. Place the hollow, bottom part of a pineapple corer in the centre of the fruit (over the core if it has one).

3. Slowly turn the handle. Be careful the corer blades don't cut the walls of the fruit. You don't want to end up with a leak!

4. Remove the flesh and put it aside, you can use this to make your drink.

The fruit will also keep your drink cooler for longer

SHAKE it UP

If you're going to master only one cocktail technique, make it the shake. The most common and iconic technique, it is as crucial to the final taste and texture of the cocktail as it is impressive to watch. Shaking the ingredients with ice combines the flavours, cools the mixture, and dilutes the drink.

1. **Add your ingredients** to a shaker. Start with your base alcohol, then balance your sweet and sour ingredients, followed by any weak elements and spices. If you don't know which ingredient is which, consult the guide on pages 34–35. Taste the mixture as you go along to ensure you have the right balance.

2. **Once you're happy** with the balance of ingredients, fill the shaker with ice cubes and close it tightly.

3. **Grasp the bottom of** the shaker with one hand and the top with the other to ensure it doesn't open mid-shake. To shake, move the shaker up and down so that the ice bounces from one end to the other. Do this for approximately 10–15 seconds.

4. **Strain the mixture** into your chosen glassware. If you're straining into a glass without ice, double strain by pouring the mixture through your fine strainer, too.

SHAKE VS SHAKE HARD

You'll see that recipes specify "shake" or "shake hard". If you're making a long drink, shake gently to bounce the ice up and down without breaking it. This cools the mixture without diluting too much and subtly combines the flavours. If you're making a short drink or a drink with fresh fruit, shake very hard so that the ice breaks in the shaker, diluting and cooling the drink and blending the flavours thoroughly.

Mix like a PRO

It doesn't end with shaking – there are plenty of other tropical cocktail techniques that cool, dilute, and combine the flavours of the drink in different ways. Sometimes these techniques are interchangeable – just like James Bond ordering his martini "shaken, not stirred".

SHAKE WITH CRUSHED ICE

Very similar to a shake with ice, but no need to strain.

1. Add all the ingredients to a shaker.
2. Fill the shaker with crushed ice.
3. Close the shaker and shake for 10–15 seconds.
4. Pour the mixture straight into your chosen glassware.

FINE BLEND

Completely combines flavours and produces a frozen drink.

1. Add all the ingredients to a blender.
2. Fill with crushed ice to the top of the liquid.
3. Blend for 20–30 seconds.
4. Pour the mixture straight into your chosen glassware.

FLASH BLEND

A partial blend. Use chunky crushed ice rather than tiny flakes.

1. Add all the ingredients to a blender.
2. Fill with crushed ice to the top of the liquid.
3. Flash blend for no more than 5 seconds.
4. Pour the mixture straight into your chosen glassware.

SWIZZLE

A stirring technique used for many iconic tropical cocktails.

1. Fill your chosen glassware with crushed ice.
2. Add all the ingredients on top.
3. Place a bar spoon in the middle of the glass and rub the spoon between your palms whilst moving it up and down inside the drink. Do this for no more than 10–15 seconds.

CHURN

A technique generally used for drinks that contain fresh fruit.

1. Add all the ingredients to your chosen serving glass.
2. Fill the glass with crushed ice.
3. Using a flat-bottomed bar spoon, churn the mixture for 10–15 seconds to move the ingredients around the glass.

MUDDLE

Extracts flavour from the solid ingredients in churned or shaken cocktails.

1. Add your diced ingredient(s) to your glassware or shaker.
2. Use a muddler or the flat end of a bar spoon to crush the ingredients to release flavour and juices.

BUILD

The simplest technique, used for drinks with 2–3 liquid ingredients.

1. Fill your glassware with ice cubes.
2. Add all the ingredients.
3. That's it!

Make it AT HOME

Homemade ingredients are a huge part of tropical cocktail history and culture. When many of the classic drinks were invented, syrups and flavourings weren't available to buy, so bartenders made these from scratch using fresh fruit and herbs. You can make many of the ingredients featured in the recipes yourself.

SUGAR SYRUPS

These mostly help to balance the sweetness of the drink, although they do have subtly different flavours, so swapping them will affect the overall taste.

SIMPLE SUGAR SYRUP

This one's a cocktail-making staple – you'll see it in many recipes.

1. Combine 1.5 parts caster sugar with 1 part boiling water.
2. Stir until the sugar has dissolved completely.

BROWN SUGAR SYRUP

Not quite as common, but a key ingredient in the Rum Punch (pp.56–57).

1. Combine 2 parts brown sugar with 1 part boiling water.
2. Stir until the sugar has dissolved completely.

HONEY WATER

Used for the Laki Lambo (pp.128–29) and the Angels' Share (pp.140–41).

1. Combine 2 parts honey with 1 part boiling water.
2. Stir until the honey has dissolved completely.

FRUIT SYRUPS

Cocktails in this book use a variety of fruit syrups, such as mango, raspberry, cherry, and passion fruit. These add both sweetness and flavour to the drink. The recipe for all of these is the same.

1. Add 1 part ripe fruit and 2 parts sugar syrup to a blender.

2. Blend until smooth

3. If the fruit has pips or seeds, strain before use.

If you're looking for commercial syrups made from natural ingredients and real fruits, Reàl Cocktail Ingredients is a great choice.

SPICED SYRUPS

As the famous punch recipe rhyme goes, add some "spice to be nice". Spiced syrups are a great way to incorporate extra flavour into a drink.

SPICED MAPLE SYRUP

This gives the Rum & Whiskey a warm, wintry flavour (pp.122–23)

1. Combine a pinch of ground cinnamon, ground cloves, and vanilla powder with 200ml (7fl oz) maple syrup.

2. Stir well.

GINGER SYRUP

See the Sexy Colada (pp.62–63) and the Tequila Sunset (pp.88–89).

1. Add 1 part fresh ginger and 2 parts sugar syrup to a blender.

2. Blend until smooth, then strain.

CINNAMON SYRUP

Used in the Nui Nui (pp.104–05) and Tiki Tiki Bang Bang (pp.126–27).

1. Break 2 cinnamon sticks into small pieces and add them to a pan with 200ml (7fl oz) sugar syrup.

2. Cook on a low heat for 5 minutes.

3. Take off the heat and leave to cool for 20 minutes, then strain.

THAI SYRUP

See the Mai Thai (pp.74–75).

1. Add 200g (7fl oz) palm sugar, 8 fresh lime leaves, and 1 stick of lemongrass to a blender.

2. Blend for 20–30 seconds or until it turns into a smooth paste.

CREAM OF THE CROP

These creamy ingredients add body and texture to the drink as well as flavour, resulting in a very indulgent and delicious cocktail!

COCONUT CREAM SYRUP

Used for the Piña Coladas (pp.60–63), this recipe will work at a pinch but Reàl Cream of Coconut will taste better!

1. Combine 2 parts sugar syrup with 1 part unsalted coconut milk.
2. Stir well.

Make the **most** of your delicious mixes – if stored in the fridge, all ingredients will keep for up to 1 month.

HONEY CREAM

Used for the Honolulu Honey (p.93).

1. Combine 1 part honey, 0.7 parts sugar, and 1 part unsalted butter.
2. Cook over a low heat and stir constantly until all the ingredients have dissolved. Don't let it boil at any point.
3. Leave to cool before use.

GARDENIA MIX

This delicious recipe was invented by Don the Beachcomber for his tiki cocktails. It is a key ingredient in the Pearl Diver (pp.90–91).

1. Combine 150g (5oz) butter, 200ml (7fl oz) honey, 80ml (2^2/$_3$fl oz) cinnamon syrup, 50ml (1^2/$_3$fl oz) pimento liqueur, and 10ml (^{1}/$_3$fl oz) vanilla paste in a big bowl.
2. Use a hand whisk to blend the mixture into a paste.

FRUIT PURÉES

Used in cocktails to add flavour and texture, these are very easy to make.

1. Ensure your fruit is fresh and ripe.
2. Wash and dice the fruit, removing any stalks and seeds.
3. Add to a blender and blend for around 20–30 seconds until you have a smooth mixture.
4. Use immediately, as the fruit will spoil quickly.

FALERNUM

This sweet, spiced liqueur is traditionally used in lots of tropical drinks. You can now find it premade, but it's also easy to make your own delicious falernum at home. In this book it features in the South Seas Daiquiri (pp.54–55), and Tropical Toffee Apple (pp.124–25).

Ingredients

200g (7oz) almond flakes

200ml (7fl oz) sugar syrup

1 tsp cloves

2 star anise

Zest of 1 lime

15ml (½fl oz) fresh ginger juice

50ml (1²/₃fl oz) Rum-Bar (or any other overproof rum)

1. Toast the almonds in a pan until golden brown.
2. Add the sugar syrup and reduce the heat, then add the cloves and star anise and cook on a low heat for 10 minutes.
3. Add the lime and ginger and remove from the heat. Leave the mixture to cool for 20 minutes.
4. Add the rum and leave to cool for 2 hours.
5. Fine strain and bottle.

Make YOUR OWN MIX

The classic punch recipe is the basis of many tropical cocktails and a foolproof method for balancing your own drinks. The recipe is 1 part sour, 2 parts sweet, 3 parts strong, 4 parts weak, and spice to be nice. Don't be afraid to get experimental – some of the best cocktails were accidents!

SWEET

This is any sweetener you add to your drink. Sweeteners can be more neutral (e.g. sugar and honey) or flavoured (e.g. fruit syrups and liqueurs). A flavoured sweetener must work with the other flavours in the drink. Syrups and liqueurs of the same flavour are largely interchangeable, but will affect the taste and strength of the drink. Syrups are sweeter and more fruity, liqueurs are alcoholic and more aromatic.

SOUR

When following the basic punch recipe, this will always be lemon or lime. Bartenders sometimes use ingredients such as Champagne, dry white wine, vinegar, or sherbet as the sour element, but these require skilled balancing. Don't expect a tasty drink if you use vinegar instead of lemon juice!

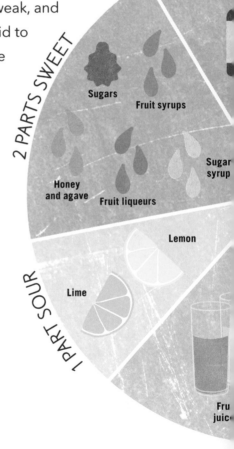

2 PARTS SWEET

Sugars

Fruit syrups

Honey and agave

Fruit liqueurs

Sugar syrup

Lemon

1 PART SOUR

Lime

Fru juic

To adapt an existing recipe, substitute ingredients in the same section to change the flavour without upsetting the balance.

3 PARTS STRONG

Spirit or other base alcohol

Coconut water

Ice

Fruit pulps and purées

4 PARTS WEAK

STRONG

This is your base alcohol (usually a spirit). You'll probably have an idea of what you want this to be, so it's usually a good starting point when choosing your ingredients. Bear in mind that some spirits are sweeter or drier than others, so balance your drink accordingly.

WEAK

This is anything non-alcoholic that isn't a concentrated sweet or sour ingredient, such as fruit juices, teas, fruit pulps and purées, coconut water, and sometimes even ice if it is used to dilute a drink (e.g. blended cocktails). Short drinks don't tend to have a weak part, but if you're making a longer drink you'll want to include this.

SPICE

Spice is more of an added bonus than an essential ingredient. This category doesn't just include typical spices like nutmeg and cinnamon – think of it as anything that seasons your drink. You can now get all sorts of spiced liqueurs, syrups, and bitters which add an extra kick of flavour. You may already have your "spice" component if you've used a spiced strong or sweet ingredient.

Angostura bitters

Cinnamon

Nutmeg

Classic GARNISHES

When you think about tropical destinations, you imagine the sea, sandy beaches, and bright fruits and flowers. Everything is colourful and mesmerizing, and this should be reflected in the presentation of your cocktails. Through colour and aroma, you can use your garnish to tell the story of the drink.

SIMPLY CITRUS

Very aromatic and versatile, citrus is probably the most common and classic cocktail garnish. Lemon or lime is used in almost every tropical cocktail.

WEDGE A very common garnish for all cocktails, sometimes intended to be squeezed into the drink. Simply cut lemons and limes into quarters lengthways for a perfect-sized wedge. You may want to cut bigger oranges into eighths.

TWIST An elegant decoration. Cut a long, thin piece of citrus peel with your peeler. Twist it around a straw or another long object to curl it.

WHEEL This citrus garnish catches the light beautifully and you can eat it. Cut a thin wheel of fruit, then cut a slit from the edge to the middle so you can slot it onto the side of your glass.

CONE This is used to hold other garnishes. Start with a wheel, then overlap the edges of the slit and pin with a cocktail stick to form a cone or bowl. You can then float this in your drink and place a flower or small fruit inside.

ZEST This adds a pop of colour to the drink and is also the most aromatic of the citrus garnishes. Simply use your zester to remove the outer layer of the fruit peel.

LEAVES & FLOWERS

You should always pick leaves and flowers that are "edible" and safe to consume, but they aren't actually intended to be eaten!

PINEAPPLE LEAVES These add height to the drink and make it look very theatrical. Simply cut them off the fruit and trim to size with scissors.

BANANA LEAVES These soft, green leaves make a great alternative to pineapple leaves. Cut them down to size and use pinking shears to get a jagged edge.

EDIBLE FLOWERS Orchids are the traditional garnish for many tropical drinks. Nowadays, you can easily buy all kinds of fresh, edible flowers online or from the supermarket. Dried flowers, such as roses, also look lovely.

FRUITY FUN

Pick a star fruit from the drink's ingredients list.

PINEAPPLE WEDGE Adds an instant tropical feel. Cut the pineapple into quarters lengthways, then slice each quarter into small triangular chunks.

FRUIT BALLS Use a melon baller on any hard fruit. The perfect, round balls will look very different to the original fruit, so your guests may not be sure what they are until they eat them!

BERRIES AND CHERRIES Placed on a cocktail stick, these dainty fruits add a welcome burst of colour.

FRUIT SLICES The size and shape of a fruit slice can really change the feel of a drink.

HERBS & SPICES

These look great and have amazing aromas.

MINT SPRIG Take a piece of the stem and leaves from the top of the plant, as this is the freshest and most visually appealing part.

LEMONGRASS STRAW Not just aromatic and attractive, it's also useful. Either peel off one layer and use as a straw or wrap a layer around a bamboo straw.

CINNAMON STICK Use this aromatic spice to skewer other garnishes. You can burn it to enhance your drink's aroma.

NUTMEG With a subtle taste and a beautiful aroma, nutmeg makes a great tropical drink topper. Simply use your grater to create a fine sprinkling, or buy ground nutmeg.

Creative GARNISHES

Sometimes a tropical drink benefits from being a little theatrical. You can experiment with combining garnishes and get as creative as you like with presentation, as long as the garnish is relevant to the drink. This doesn't mean it should look like a fruit salad – sometimes less is more!

APPLE FAN

A seriously impressive, yet easy-to-make, garnish.

1. Cut the apple in half just before the core.

2. Cut the half into slices, keeping them all together.

3. Skewer one end of the slices with a cocktail stick.

4. Spread the slices out at the other end to make a fan.

ORANGE FEATHER

This embellished orange twist decorates the Nui Nui (pp.104–05).

1. Use a peeler to cut a long, wide piece of orange peel.

2. Cut 45° slits along one side to make a feather effect.

3. Wrap the peel around a straw so that the feathered side sticks out.

CRUSHED ICE BOWL

Used to hold the rose petals in the Lanai Punch (pp.136–37), this is a great way to display garnishes in a glass. You just need crushed ice and a citrus press.

1. Fill the citrus press with crushed ice.

2. Squeeze the press together very hard.

3. Open. The ice should have compressed into a bowl shape.

4. Place this in your drink and fill with garnishes.

SALT RIM

This will also work with sugar and spices. You can coat just one side of the rim so that guests can choose whether to drink through it.

1. Rub the rim of the glass with lemon or lime.
2. Pour the salt onto a small plate and dip the rim into it, twisting to get an even coverage. Remove.
3. Clean the inside of the rim to prevent the salt from falling into the drink and offsetting the balance.

PINEAPPLE BIRD

This is a great example of using a garnish to tell a story. The bird reflects the name of the drink and the ingredients in the Jungle Bird (pp.80–81).

1. Cut off the top of the pineapple with a couple of centimetres of the flesh and the leaves.
2. Cut the top into eighths, lengthways.
3. Rotate, so that the curve of the pineapple resembles the head and back of a bird and the feathers look like a long, feathered tail.
4. Push a short cocktail stick into the head and attach a glacé cherry to make the beak.

FRUIT WEB

Cut thin sticks of hard fruits, such as apple or rhubarb, and layer them across the top of the drink. You can then balance other garnishes on top of this sturdy frame (see English Tea-Ki Garden, pp.132–33).

COCKTAIL STICKS

The humble cocktail stick is your best friend when it comes to drink presentation. Simply skewer different garnishes onto one stick (see Jamaican Punch, pp.58–59), or use the stick to integrate the garnishes (see Sex on the Beach, pp.110–11) – the possibilities are endless!

Sharing is CARING

Sharing cocktails are big in the tropical cocktail world.
You can drink them together with long straws or ladle them
into smaller cups. The recipe should be a crowd-pleaser,
so it's best to choose a long, refreshing drink with
popular ingredients – the Angels' Share
(pp.140–41) is the perfect example.

THE RECIPE

Follow these simple steps to turn
any long cocktail into a sharer:

1. Check the ingredients
   list. Swap any fresh fruit
   for fresh juice to avoid
   having to muddle.

2. Multiply the ingredient
   quantities by the number
   of servings you want.
   Add a little extra alcohol
   as sharing drinks will
   dilute quickly on ice.

3. Pour the mixture into a
   punch bowl filled with ice.

4. Swizzle the mixture for
   no more than 20 seconds,
   moving your swizzle tool
   around the bowl to mix all
   ingredients thoroughly.

We drink with all our senses, so make sure your sharer looks as amazing as it tastes. Use a beautiful punch bowl and garnish extravagantly.

TOP SHARERS

The cocktails below make great sharing cocktails – they are full of delicious, popular ingredients, and are particularly easy to scale up.

JAMAICAN PUNCH
(pp.58–59)

ORCHIDEA
(pp.84–85)

ROYAL PALACE MOJITO
(pp.102–03)

RUM RUNNER
(pp.114–15)

SWIZZLE WITH STYLE

You can swizzle with a regular bar spoon, but the molinillo is the perfect theatrical tool. Originally used for chocolate drinks, it dates back to 16th-century Latin America. The grooves and holes help mix the ingredients efficiently and smoothly.

Top 10 QUICK WINS

You may want to spend time mastering some of the more advanced cocktails in this book, but if you're in a rush or planning a cocktail evening with a lot of guests, it's always handy to have a few go-to easy recipes. Here's a selection of the top 10 quick and easy tropical recipes for every occasion.

1. TROPICAIPIRINHA

(pp.48–49) With only four ingredients, this is one of the easiest twists to master in this book – yet it couldn't be more deliciously tropical.

2. QUEEN'S PARK SWIZZLE

(pp.50–51) This eye-catching drink looks sophisticated and impressive, but it is secretly really easy to make.

3. DAIQUIRI

(pp.52–53) The ultimate example of delicious simplicity – you only need three ingredients. You can also add fresh fruit and blend with crushed ice for a fruity twist.

4. RUM PUNCH

(pp.56–57) Simple and classic, the Rum Punch is a great crowd-pleaser and the ingredients won't break the bank.

5. JUNGLE BIRD

(pp.80–81) For a tiki cocktail, the Jungle Bird is a surprisingly simple drink. The wow factor comes from the theatrical garnish.

6. MARGARITA

(pp.82–83) Another three-ingredient wonder, this classic drink also works well blended with crushed ice and fresh fruit.

7. TEQUILA SUNRISE

(pp.86–87) A disco-era classic cocktail, this drink is fantastically easy to make en masse if you're hosting a big party.

8. HURRICANE

(pp.96–97) It looks impressive and it tastes great, but you can whip up this tropical classic with only four ingredients.

9. SEX ON THE BEACH

(pp.110–11) Delicious and uncomplicated, this cheeky 1980s cocktail is a great choice for those who prefer a more neutral base spirit.

10. WIKI TIKI

(pp.138–39) This one takes the prize for the most interesting, yet easily achievable, modern tropical cocktail.

From simple, delicious **Caribbean** recipes to **spectacular tiki** concoctions, the classics have a **lot to offer.** Some you'll be able to whip up in no time, and others will really test your new **bartending skills**. You can even **learn how** to put a spin on the original recipes with the **creative twists.**

CLASSIC COCKTAILS
&TWISTS

CAIPIRINHA

The Caipirinha started life as a 20th century flu medicine. The original recipe combined aguardiente (a Portuguese term for distilled alcohol) with lemon, honey, and garlic. When aguardiente was substituted for cachaça, the lemon for lime, and garlic and honey for sugar, the national drink of Brazil was born. You can replace the cachaça with vodka to make a Caipiroska. With rum, it is called a Caipirissima.

THE CLASSIC RECIPE

Super simple and delicious, the Caipirinha is one of the best-known and loved tropical cocktails.

1. Lightly muddle ½ diced lime and 2 tsp sugar in a rocks glass to release the lime juice and dissolve the sugar. Don't overdo this, as the skin of the lime can leave a bitter taste when crushed.
2. Fill the glass with crushed ice and add 50ml (1²/₃fl oz) cachaça.
3. Churn for approximately 10 seconds.
4. Top with extra crushed ice.

Serve in a rocks glass

Cachaça

Sugar

Lime

EXTRAS

THE SIGNATURE GARNISH for this drink is a lime wedge.

TURN OVER FOR REINVENTIONS ▶

CAIPIRINHA REINVENTED

50ml (1²/₃fl oz) cachaça
½ passion fruit
⅛ diced lime
20ml (²/₃fl oz) mango syrup

TROPICAIPIRINHA

A fruity twist with extra tropical flavours. To make mango syrup, see page 31. Lightly muddle the mango syrup, diced lime, and passion fruit in a rocks glass. Add the cachaça and fill the rest of the glass with crushed ice. Churn well and top with extra crushed ice. Garnish with a lime wedge and a ½ passion fruit.

10ml (¹/₃fl oz) Campari
25ml (⁴/₆fl oz) sloe gin
25ml (¹/₅fl oz) gin
1 tsp caster sugar
½ passion fruit
2 slices orange
½ diced lime

CAIPIRINELLA

A tempting variation with a gin base. Lightly muddle the lime, orange, passion fruit, and sugar in a rocks glass. Add the gin, sloe gin, and Campari. Fill the rest of the glass with crushed ice. Churn for approximately 10 seconds, then top with extra crushed ice. Garnish with a lime wedge.

LOSE THE BOOZE

50ml (1²/₃fl oz) coconut water
50ml (1²/₃fl oz) pineapple juice
25ml (⁴/₅fl oz) sugar syrup
½ diced lime

PIÑA CAIPIRINHA

A delicious mocktail twist. Lightly muddle the lime and sugar syrup in a highball glass. Add the pineapple juice, coconut water, and fill the rest of the glass with crushed ice. Churn and top with extra crushed ice. Garnish with a lime wedge, pineapple leaf, and coconut flakes.

Queen's Park SWIZZLE

The Queen's Park Hotel in Trinidad opened its doors in 1895 and this classic cocktail was likely invented soon after. In its time, the hotel was at the heart of the tropical cocktail scene. If there hadn't been the rise of Cuban cocktail culture in the 1920s and the worldwide promotion of the Mojito by Bacardi, we would probably be drinking more Queen's Park Swizzles today.

THE CLASSIC RECIPE

The finished drink should have three eye-catching layers of colour.

1. Swizzle 50ml (1²/₃fl oz) gold rum, 20ml (²/₃fl oz) lime juice, 5–6 mint leaves, 2 tsp soft demerara sugar, and crushed ice in a highball glass.

2. Top with 4–6 dashes of Angostura bitters. This gives the drink a splash of colour and aroma while the flavour mixes into the drink.

Angostura bitters

Lime juice

Soft demerara sugar

Mint leaves

Serve in a highball glass

Gold rum

EXTRAS

DECORATE your drink with a simple mint sprig or a single lime wedge.

DAIQUIRI

This drink was invented in the early 1900s, when an American mine engineer, Jennings Cox, was serving drinks to his workers in the Daiquiri region of Cuba. Rumour has it that Jennings ran out of gin, so he started shaking cocktails with white rum instead – introducing the now iconic trio of rum, lime, and sugar. Everyone loved the combination of flavours, and the Daiquiri was born.

THE CLASSIC RECIPE

The beauty of this classic drink is the simplicity of its ingredients.

1. Add 50ml (1²/₃fl oz) white rum, 15ml (¹/₂fl oz) sugar syrup, and 20ml (²/₃fl oz) lime juice to a shaker.
2. Fill the shaker with ice and shake hard.
3. Fine strain into a chilled coupe glass.

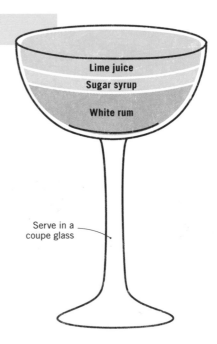

Lime juice

Sugar syrup

White rum

Serve in a coupe glass

EXTRAS

BALANCE AN elegant lime wedge on the side of the glass.

TURN OVER FOR REINVENTIONS ▶

DAIQUIRI REINVENTED

20ml (²/₃fl oz)
lime juice

10ml (¹/₃fl oz)
passion fruit syrup

10ml (¹/₃fl oz)
falernum

50ml (1²/₃fl oz)
white rum

1 pineapple ring

SOUTH SEAS DAIQUIRI

A twist using the traditional tropical liqueur, falernum (see p.33 to make it at home). Muddle the pineapple in the bottom of a shaker. Add the rum, falernum, passion fruit syrup, and lime juice. Shake hard with ice and fine strain into a chilled coupe glass. Garnish with a lime twist and a dash of Angostura bitters.

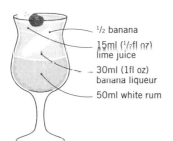

¹/₂ banana

15ml (¹/₂fl oz)
lime juice

30ml (1fl oz)
banana liqueur

50ml white rum

BANANA DAIQUIRI

A tempting guilty pleasure created in the 1950s. Blend all the ingredients with a scoop of crushed ice. Pour into a chilled coupe glass and garnish with a banana slice and a glacé cherry.

15ml (¹/₂fl oz) pink
grapefruit juice

7.5ml (¹/₄fl oz)
lime juice

10ml (¹/₃fl oz)
maraschino liqueur

50ml (1²/₃fl oz)
gold rum

HEMINGWAY DAIQUIRI

This twist was invented for the famous American author, Ernest Hemingway. Add all the ingredients to a shaker. Fill with ice and shake hard. Fine strain into a chilled coupe glass. Garnish with a lime wedge.

Rum PUNCH

You can't get much more classic than a punch. The drink was brought to England from India in the 17th century by sailors, and soon gained popularity throughout Europe. By the mid-1650s imports of Jamaican rum had established the famous Caribbean Rum Punch recipe given below. The balance of ingredients follows the simple rhyme, "1 of sour, 2 of sweet, 3 of strong, 4 of weak, and spice to be nice".

THE CLASSIC RECIPE

With only a handful of delicious ingredients, this is one of the easiest tropical cocktails to make at home.

1. Add 45ml (1½fl oz) aged rum, 30ml (1fl oz) brown sugar syrup, 15ml (½fl oz) lime juice, and 60ml (2fl oz) coconut water to a rocks glass filled with ice cubes.

2. Top your drink with a sprinkle of grated nutmeg.

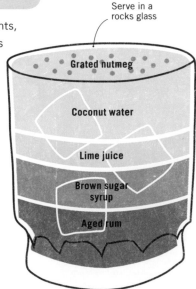

Serve in a rocks glass

Grated nutmeg

Coconut water

Lime juice

Brown sugar syrup

Aged rum

LOSE THE BOOZE

For a light, non-alcoholic alternative, simply swap the rum for your favourite flavour of tea.

EXTRAS

THIS CLASSIC drink wouldn't be complete without a lime wedge garnish.

TURN OVER FOR REINVENTIONS ▶

RUM PUNCH REINVENTED

35ml (1¹/₅fl oz)
pineapple juice

35ml (1¹/₅fl oz)
orange juice

15ml (¹/₂fl oz)
lime juice

20ml (²/₃fl oz) grenadine

50ml (1²/₃fl oz)
Jamaican aged rum

JAMAICAN PUNCH

This popular recipe uses iconic flavours from the Caribbean island. Shake all the ingredients with ice and strain into a rocks glass filled with ice cubes. Garnish with an orange wheel, 3 pineapple leaves, and a glacé cherry on a cocktail stick.

20ml (²/₃fl oz)
orange Juice

30ml (1fl oz)
Earl Grey tea

10ml (¹/₃fl oz)
lime juice

15ml (¹/₂fl oz)
natural agave nectar

2 dashes of
Angostura bitters

50ml (1²/₃fl oz)
Jamaican aged rum

GROG O'CLOCK

Tea gives this variation a delicate flavour. Shake all the ingredients with ice and strain into a rocks glass filled with ice cubes. Garnish with an orange wheel, a lime wedge, and a glacé cherry on a cocktail stick.

Piña COLADA

Created in 1954 in Puerto Rico's Caribe Hilton bar by Ramón Marrero, the Piña Colada is an example of how one cocktail can boost tourism for a whole island. Tourists still go to the hotel just to try the famous drink. One of the most influential cocktails in the world, it is used as a fragrance and flavour in many products, and there is even a Piña Colada song.

THE CLASSIC RECIPE

A high-quality coconut cream syrup is crucial, see page 32 to make it at home.

1. Place 60ml (2fl oz) Puerto Rican gold rum, 1 dash of Angostura bitters, 30ml (1/2fl oz) cream of coconut syrup (Reàl), 5ml (1/6fl oz) lime juice, and 40ml (1 1/3fl oz) fresh pineapple juice in a blender.
2. Fill the blender with crushed ice and a few ice cubes up to the top of the liquid, then blend for 20–30 seconds.
3. Pour into a poco grande glass.

Fresh pineapple juice

Lime juice

Cream of coconut syrup (Reàl)

Angostura bitters

Puerto Rican gold rum

Serve in a poco grande glass

EXTRAS

GARNISH with a pineapple wedge, a glacé cherry, and pineapple leaves.

TURN OVER FOR REINVENTIONS ▸

PIÑA COLADA REINVENTED

- A few dashes of Angostura bitters
- Grated nutmeg
- Pinch of salt
- 25ml (⁴/₅fl oz) coconut water
- 50ml (1⅔fl oz) pineapple juice
- 15ml (½fl oz) lime juice
- 10ml (⅓fl oz) ginger syrup
- 30ml (1fl oz) cream of coconut syrup (Reàl)
- 60ml (2fl oz) Puerto Rican gold rum

SEXY COLADA

Here, this Daniele Dalla Pola recipe is blended rather than shaken. Blend the rum, cream of coconut syrup (Reàl), ginger syrup, lime juice, pineapple juice, coconut water, and salt with crushed ice. Pour into a poco grande glass. Top with the Angostura bitters and grated nutmeg. Garnish with pineapple leaves, a glacé cherry, and an orchid.

- 80ml (2⅔fl oz) orange juice
- 20ml (⅔fl oz) lime juice
- 30ml (1fl oz) cream of coconut syrup (Reàl)
- 10ml (⅓fl oz) grenadine
- 15ml (½fl oz) crème de cacao white
- 25ml (⁴/₅fl oz) coconut rum liqueur
- 25ml (⁴/₅fl oz) gold rum

COCO KANE

A seriously coconut-flavoured twist on the classic. Shake all the ingredients with ice and strain into a poco grande glass filled with ice cubes. Top with crushed ice and garnish with pineapple leaves, a cherry, and coconut shavings.

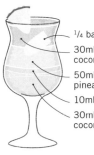

LOSE THE BOOZE

- ¼ banana
- 30ml (1fl oz) coconut water
- 50ml (1⅔fl oz) pineapple juice
- 10ml (⅓fl oz) lime juice
- 30ml (1fl oz) cream of coconut syrup (Reàl)

VIRGIN COLADA

A variation with all of the flavour but none of the booze. Add all the ingredients to a blender. Fill the blender with crushed ice up to the top of the liquid, then blend for 20–30 seconds. Pour into a poco grande glass, and garnish with a pineapple wedge.

Pornstar MARTINI

This cheeky modern classic was created in 1999 by Douglas Ankrah of London's Lab bar. Later, Ankrah opened iconic London bar, Townhouse. Although both ventures have now sadly closed, the two bars inspired bartenders for over a decade. The Pornstar Martini should be served with a shot of Champagne (or other sparkling wine) on the side to cleanse your palate and balance the drink.

THE CLASSIC RECIPE

You can make the passion fruit purée at home (see p.33).

1. Add 40ml (1¹/₃fl oz) vanilla vodka, 12.5ml (²/₅fl oz) Passoa liqueur, 30ml (1fl oz) passion fruit purée, and 2 tsp vanilla sugar to a shaker.
2. Fill the shaker with ice and shake hard, then fine strain into a chilled martini glass.
3. Serve with a shot of Champagne.

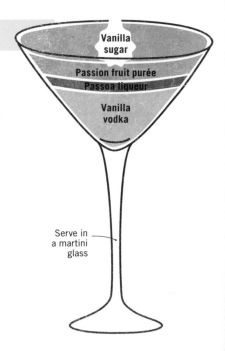

Vanilla sugar

Passion fruit purée
Passoa liqueur

Vanilla vodka

Serve in a martini glass

EXTRAS

THE SIGNATURE GARNISH for this drink is a floating 1/2 passion fruit.

Singapore SLING

One of the most delicious, refreshing, and advanced cocktails for its time, the Singapore Sling was created at the Raffles Hotel's Long Bar, Singapore, around 1915 by Ngiam Tong Boon. This drink predates tiki-style cocktails but it is often mistaken for one because of its complexity.

THE CLASSIC RECIPE

A delightfully boozy cocktail that slips down easily – drink with caution!

1. Muddle 1 pineapple ring in the bottom of a shaker.
2. Add 50ml (1²/₃fl oz) gin, 15ml (¹/₂fl oz) Cointreau, 15ml (¹/₂fl oz) Cherry Heering, 10ml (¹/₃fl oz) Benedictine, a dash of Angostura bitters, a dash of orange bitters, 15ml (¹/₂fl oz) grenadine, and 20ml (²/₃fl oz) lemon juice to the shaker.
3. Fill the shaker with ice, shake hard, then strain into a sling glass filled with ice cubes.
4. Top with soda.

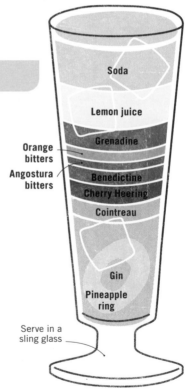

Soda

Lemon juice

Grenadine

Orange bitters

Angostura bitters

Benedictine

Cherry Heering

Cointreau

Gin

Pineapple ring

Serve in a sling glass

EXTRAS

GARNISH with a pineapple wedge and a lemon wedge, or a fresh cherry.

TURN OVER FOR REINVENTIONS ▶

SINGAPORE SLING REINVENTED

- 30ml (1fl oz) soda
- 25ml (⁴/₅fl oz) lemon juice
- 20ml (²/₃fl oz) cherry syrup (Real)
- 1 dash of Angostura bitters
- 15ml (½fl oz) Benedictine
- 20ml (²/₃fl oz) dark rum
- 30ml (1fl oz) gin
- 1 pineapple ring

TIKI SING SLING

The addition of rum gives the classic recipe a tiki twist. Muddle the pineapple ring in the bottom of a shaker. Add the rest of the ingredients apart from the soda. Fill with ice and shake hard. Strain into a highball glass filled with ice cubes. Garnish with a lemon twist and a fresh cherry.

- 20ml (²/₃fl oz) ginger ale
- 20ml (²/₃fl oz) orange juice
- 20ml (²/₃fl oz) lemon juice
- 1 dash of Angostura bitters
- 15ml (½fl oz) Grand Marnier Cherry
- 15ml (½fl oz) Grand Marnier
- 15ml (½fl oz) Drambuie
- 40ml (1¹/₃fl oz) Scotch

SCOTTISH SLING

A modern twist using Scotch as the base alcohol. Add all the ingredients apart from the ginger ale to a shaker. Fill with ice, then shake. Strain into a sling glass filled with ice cubes. Top with ginger ale and garnish with orange zest or a cherry liqueur chocolate.

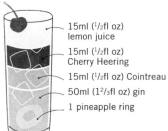

- 15ml (½fl oz) lemon juice
- 15ml (½fl oz) Cherry Heering
- 15ml (½fl oz) Cointreau
- 50ml (1²/₃fl oz) gin
- 1 pineapple ring

SINGAPORE SLANG

A simplified version of the Singapore Sling. Muddle the pineapple ring in the bottom of a shaker, then add the rest of the ingredients. Fill with ice and shake hard. Strain into a slim highball glass filled with ice cubes. Garnish with a fresh cherry.

Blue HAWAII

This cocktail was created in 1957 at the legendary Hilton Hawaiian Village hotel by head bartender Harry Yee. The recipe was very innovative at the time, as there were not many blue drinks around. The Blue Hawaii really put blue Curaçao on the map. Yee was also the first person to use cocktail umbrellas and orchids as garnishes.

THE CLASSIC RECIPE

A big glass shows off the striking colour of this drink.

1. Muddle 1 pineapple ring in a shaker.
2. Fill the shaker with ice and add 50ml (1²/₃fl oz) white rum, 25ml (⁴/₅fl oz) blue Curaçao, 20ml (²/₃fl oz) coconut rum, 5ml (¹/₆fl oz) sugar syrup, and 20ml (²/₃fl oz) lime juice.
3. Shake hard and strain into a hurricane glass filled with ice cubes.
4. Top with lemonade.

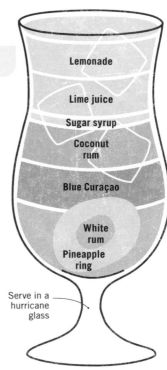

Lemonade

Lime juice

Sugar syrup

Coconut rum

Blue Curaçao

White rum

Pineapple ring

Serve in a hurricane glass

EXTRAS

COMPLETE your
drink with a thin
pineapple wedge
garnish and an orchid.

Mai TAI

In 1944 Victor Jules Bergeron Jr., founder of the Polynesian "tiki" restaurant Trader Vic's, mixed a cocktail using 17-year-old Wray & Nephew rum, orange Curaçao, orgeat syrup, fresh lime juice, and rock candy syrup to serve to some friends from Tahiti. Their verdict was "Mai tai-roa aé!" ("Out of this world!") – and the legendary Mai Tai was born.

THE CLASSIC RECIPE

As 17-year-old Wray & Nephew rum is no longer produced, the classic Mai Tai now uses agricole and Jamaican rums.

1. Add 30ml (1fl oz) Jamaican aged rum, 30ml (1fl oz) aged agricole rum, 15ml (1/2fl oz) orange Curaçao, 10ml (1/3fl oz) orgeat syrup, 25ml (4/5fl oz) lime juice, and 1 tsp soft brown sugar to a shaker.
2. Fill the shaker with ice, shake hard, then strain into a rocks glass filled with ice cubes.

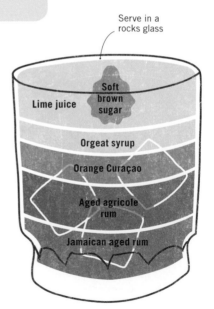

Serve in a rocks glass

Lime juice

Soft brown sugar

Orgeat syrup

Orange Curaçao

Aged agricole rum

Jamaican aged rum

EXTRAS

POSITION a ¹/₂ lime and a mint sprig on top to look like an island with a palm tree.

TURN OVER FOR REINVENTIONS ▸

MAI TAI REINVENTED

25ml (⁴/₅fl oz) lime juice
20ml (²/₃fl oz) Thai syrup
15ml (¹/₂fl oz) Cointreau
50ml (1²/₃fl oz) gold rum

MAI THAI

You can make the Thai syrup yourself (see p.31). Combine all ingredients in a shaker. Fill the shaker with ice and shake hard. Strain into a rocks glass filled with ice cubes. Top with crushed ice, lime zest, a fresh lime leaf, and a lemongrass stick straw.

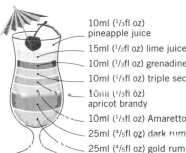

10ml (¹/₃fl oz) pineapple juice
15ml (¹/₂fl oz) lime juice
10ml (¹/₃fl oz) grenadine
10ml (¹/₃fl oz) triple sec
10ml (¹/₃fl oz) apricot brandy
10ml (¹/₃fl oz) Amaretto
25ml (⁴/₅fl oz) dark rum
25ml (⁴/₅fl oz) gold rum

DISCO MAI TAI

A popular 1980s take on the traditional Mai Tai. Combine all ingredients in a shaker. Fill the shaker with ice and shake. Strain into a hurricane glass filled with crushed ice. Garnish with slices of pineapple, a glacé cherry, and an umbrella.

20ml (²/₃fl oz) lime juice

LOSE THE BOOZE

15ml (¹/₂fl oz) orgeat syrup
1 tsp soft brown sugar
30ml (1fl oz) pineapple juice
50ml (1²/₃fl oz) orange juice

INNOCENT MAI TAI

A delicious mocktail variation of the classic. Combine all ingredients in a shaker. Fill the shaker with ice and shake hard. Strain into a rocks glass filled with ice cubes. Garnish with a mint sprig and a ball of almond ice cream.

Fog CUTTER

Like the Mai Tai, this is an original 1940s Trader Vic's tiki cocktail. Very advanced for its time, it showed that a number of different base spirits could be used together in one drink. The result is a potent but truly delicious combination. As Trader Vic noted, "Fog Cutter, hell. After two of these, you won't even see the stuff".

THE CLASSIC RECIPE

The light citrus flavour cuts through the seriously alcoholic base.

1. Add 40ml (1¹/₃fl oz) gold rum, 15ml (¹/₂fl oz) Cognac, 10ml (¹/₃fl oz) gin, 15ml (¹/₂fl oz) orgeat syrup, 20ml (²/₃fl oz) lemon juice, and 30ml (1fl oz) orange juice to a shaker.
2. Fill the shaker with ice, then shake.
3. Strain into a highball glass filled with ice cubes.
4. Pour over 15ml (¹/₂fl oz) cream sherry.

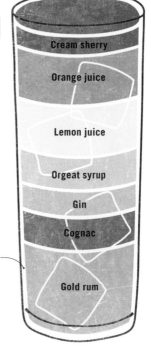

Cream sherry

Orange juice

Lemon juice

Orgeat syrup

Gin

Cognac

Serve in a highball glass

Gold rum

LOSE THE
BOOZE

Replace the alcohol with 40ml (1¹/₃fl oz) black tea, 20ml (²/₃fl oz) grape juice, and a dash of orange blossom water.

EXTRAS

AN ORANGE
twist wrapped around a mint sprig makes a fun but elegant garnish.

TURN OVER FOR REINVENTIONS ▶

FOG CUTTER REINVENTED

- 40ml (1⅓fl oz) apple juice
- 25ml (⅘fl oz) lemon juice
- 15ml (½fl oz) elderflower cordial
- 15ml (½fl oz) passion fruit syrup
- 15ml (½fl oz) dark rum
- 10ml (⅓fl oz) Cognac
- 40ml (1⅓fl oz) gin

LONDON FOG CUTTER

Try making your own passion fruit syrup (see p.31). Gosling's Black Seal rum is particularly good in this. Combine all the ingredients in a shaker. Fill the shaker with ice and shake. Strain into a sling glass filled with ice cubes. Garnish with an apple fan (see p.38) and a glacé cherry.

- Pulp of 1 passion fruit
- 40ml (1⅓fl oz) mandarin juice
- 20ml (⅔fl oz) lemon juice
- 10ml (⅓fl oz) orgeat syrup
- 1 dash of orange blossom water
- 20ml (⅔fl oz) muscat desert wine
- 20ml (⅔fl oz) Chilean pisco
- 20ml (⅔fl oz) gin
- 20ml (⅔fl oz) white rum

MURKY MORNING

An exotic variation of the Fog Cutter. Combine all the ingredients in a shaker. Fill the shaker with ice and shake. Strain into a sling glass filled with ice cubes. Garnish with an orange cone and 3 grapes on a cocktail stick.

- 30ml (1fl oz) orange juice
- 20ml (⅔fl oz) lemon juice
- 10ml (⅓fl oz) sugar syrup
- 15ml (½fl oz) orgeat
- 20ml (⅔fl oz) Cognac
- 40ml (1⅓fl oz) gold rum

FINEST CUT

A simplified version of the Fog Cutter for a quick win. Combine all the ingredients in a shaker. Fill the shaker with ice and shake. Strain into a rocks glass filled with ice cubes. Garnish with an orange twist and glacé cherry.

Jungle BIRD

This tiki-style cocktail was created in 1978 in the Hilton Hotel's Aviary Bar in Kuala Lumpur. With a simpler combination of base ingredients than most tiki drinks, it's like a tropical version of a classic Negroni. This is a great cocktail to choose if you want to brush up your presentation skills and get creative with your garnish.

THE CLASSIC RECIPE

Sweet pineapple juice balances the bitter Campari and lime.

1. Pour 50ml (1²/₃fl oz) Jamaican aged rum, 20ml (²/₃fl oz) Campari, 10ml (¹/₃fl oz) sugar syrup, 15ml (¹/₂fl oz) lime juice, and 50ml (1²/₃fl oz) pineapple juice into a shaker.
2. Fill the shaker with ice, shake hard, then strain into a rocks glass filled with ice cubes.

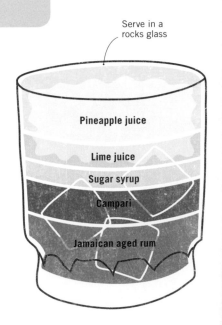

Serve in a rocks glass

Pineapple juice

Lime juice

Sugar syrup

Campari

Jamaican aged rum

EXTRAS

TRY MAKING a cute pineapple "jungle bird" to perch on the side of your drink (see p.39).

MARGARITA

Tequila gained popularity during the Prohibition era, when many Americans travelled to Mexico to satisfy their thirst for spirits. The first recipe for a Margarita appeared in the 1940s and used a simple combination of tequila, orange liqueur, and lime. The trend for adding salt on the rim of the glass came later, as did the vogue for frozen Margaritas and fruity Margaritas.

THE CLASSIC RECIPE

See page 39 to learn how to give your drink a salty kick with a coarse salt rim.

1. Pour 60ml (2fl oz) white tequila, 20ml (²/₃fl oz) Cointreau, and 20ml (²/₃fl oz) lime juice into a shaker.
2. Fill the shaker with ice, shake hard, then strain into a chilled margarita glass.

Lime juice

Cointreau

White tequila

Serve in a margarita glass

EXTRAS

A LIME WEDGE
garnish is all
that's needed
to complete the
perfect Margarita.

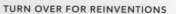

TURN OVER FOR REINVENTIONS ▶

MARGARITA REINVENTED

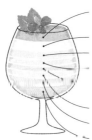

15ml (½fl oz) clementine juice

15ml (½fl oz) pineapple juice

15ml (½fl oz) lime juice

10ml (⅓fl oz) orgeat syrup

10ml (⅓fl oz) natural agave nectar

10ml (⅓fl oz) Cointreau

15ml (½fl oz) mezcal

35ml (1⅕fl oz) white tequila

ORCHIDEA

The sweet agave syrup balances the citrus flavours. Add all the ingredients to a brandy balloon or wide rocks glass filled with crushed ice. Swizzle, and top with more crushed ice. Garnish with an orchid and a mint sprig.

1 slice of pineapple

1 slice of watermelon

20ml (⅔fl oz) lime juice

15ml (½fl oz) sugar syrup

20ml (⅔fl oz) Cointreau

60ml (2fl oz) white tequila

TEQUILA ON THE BEACH

A summery, fruity variation on the classic Margarita. Blend all the ingredients with a scoop of crushed ice. Pour into a chilled margarita glass and garnish with a lime wedge.

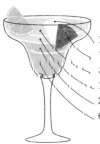

20ml (⅔fl oz) pink grapefruit juice

10ml (⅓fl oz) lime juice

10ml (⅓fl oz) grenadine

5ml (⅙fl oz) maraschino cherry liqueur

15ml (½fl oz) Cointreau

50ml (1⅔fl oz) aged tequila

1 pineapple ring

PINK MERRY

Grenadine and cherries turn a classic pink. Muddle the pineapple ring in the bottom of a shaker. Add the remaining ingredients, fill the shaker with ice, and shake hard. Strain into a chilled martini glass and garnish with a small pineapple wedge.

Tequila SUNRISE

The first recipe, created in the 1930s by Gene Sulit in Phoenix, Arizona, comprised tequila, lime juice, crème de cassis, and soda water. The recipe we know today was created in the early 1970s by bartenders Bobby Lazoff and Billy Rice at The Trident, a music and party venue in Sausalito, California. The Rolling Stones popularized the drink after sampling it at The Trident during their 1972 US tour.

THE CLASSIC RECIPE

Once you've admired the cocktail's sunrise layers, stir before drinking.

1. Fill a highball glass with ice cubes.
2. Add 50ml (1²/₃fl oz) aged tequila and 120ml (4fl oz) orange juice, then stir.
3. Slowly pour 15ml (¹/₂fl oz) grenadine on the top.

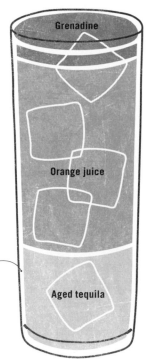

Grenadine

Orange juice

Serve in a highball glass

Aged tequila

EXTRAS

THE ORANGE
wheel and glacé
cherry garnish is
designed to look
like the rising sun.

TURN OVER FOR REINVENTIONS ▶

TEQUILA SUNRISE REINVENTED

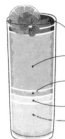

- 15ml (½fl oz) crème de cassis
- 80ml (2⅔fl oz) orange juice
- 10ml (⅓fl oz) ginger syrup
- 10ml (⅓fl oz) natural agave nectar
- 50ml (1⅔fl oz) white tequila

TEQUILA SUNSET

You can make the ginger syrup at home (see p.31), or you can use ginger liqueur if you prefer. Combine all the ingredients except the crème de cassis in a shaker. Fill the shaker with ice, shake for 10 seconds, then strain into a large highball glass filled with crushed ice. Slowly pour the crème de cassis on top. Garnish with an orange cone and an orchid.

- 15ml (½fl oz) crème de mûre
- 30ml (1fl oz) orange juice
- 10ml (⅓fl oz) lemon juice
- 15ml (½fl oz) lime juice
- 10ml (⅓fl oz) orgeat syrup
- 15ml (½fl oz) natural agave nectar
- 50ml (1⅔fl oz) mezcal

OAXACA SUNRISE

The mezcal gives a lovely smoky flavour to this Sunrise. Combine all the ingredients except the crème de mûre in a shaker. Fill the shaker with ice, shake for 10 seconds, then strain into a sling glass filled with ice cubes. Slowly pour the crème de mûre on top. Garnish with an orange wedge and a cherry.

Pearl DIVER

A less well-known cocktail from tiki creator Don the Beachcomber than some of his other innovations, this cocktail is nevertheless one of the most delicious. Its blend of rums, spices, butter, honey, and citrus is a wonderful combination. Developed in the 1950s, it is actually a twist on one of his earlier recipes, the Pearl Diver Punch.

THE CLASSIC RECIPE

It's best to make the gardenia mix yourself (see p.32).

1. Place 40ml (1¹/₃fl oz) gold rum, 20ml (²/₃fl oz) Jamaican aged rum, 1 dash of Angostura bitters, 20ml (²/₃fl oz) gardenia mix, 10ml (¹/₃fl oz) lime juice, and 20ml (²/₃fl oz) orange juice in a blender and blend for 10 seconds to dissolve the gardenia mix.
2. Add crushed ice up to the top of the liquid and flash blend for no more than 5 seconds.
3. Pour into a pearl diver glass.

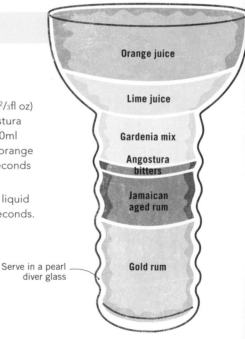

Orange juice

Lime juice

Gardenia mix

Angostura bitters

Jamaican aged rum

Gold rum

Serve in a pearl diver glass

EXTRAS

COMPLETE the tropical effect by garnishing with a banana leaf and an orchid.

TURN OVER FOR REINVENTIONS

PEARL DIVER REINVENTED

20ml (²/₃fl oz) mandarin juice

20ml (²/₃fl oz) gardenia mix

10ml (¹/₃fl oz) dry Curaçao

50ml (1²/₃fl oz) Pusser's original rum

JEWEL OF THE SEA

You can make the gardenia mix yourself (see p.32). Combine all the ingredients in a shaker. Fill the shaker with ice, shake for 10 seconds, then strain into a rocks glass or shell mug filled with ice cubes. Garnish with a large orchid.

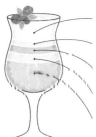

40ml (1¹/₃fl oz) pineapple juice

15ml (¹/₂fl oz) lime juice

20ml (²/₃fl oz) mango purée

20ml (²/₃fl oz) honey cream

50ml (1²/₃fl oz) Puerto Rican gold rum

HONOLULU HONEY

Make the mango purée yourself (see p.33). Combine all the ingredients in a shaker. Fill the shaker with ice, shake for 10 seconds, then strain into a tiki mug or a poco grande glass filled with crushed ice. Garnish with an orchid.

Blue LAGOON

This classic cocktail was created in the late 1960s by Andy MacElhone (son of legendary bartender Harry MacElhone) at Harry's New York Bar in Paris. Most modern recipes use vodka, blue Curaçao, and lemonade, but the original used homemade lemonade for a more citrussy kick.

THE CLASSIC RECIPE

Visually stunning, this cocktail is also deliciously tangy and refreshing.

1. Pour 40ml (1¹/₃fl oz) vodka, 30ml (1fl oz) blue Curaçao, 15ml (¹/₂fl oz) sugar syrup, and 25ml (⁴/₅fl oz) lemon juice into a shaker.
2. Fill the shaker with crushed ice up to the top of the liquid and shake hard.
3. Pour into a sling glass and top with 20ml (²/₃fl oz) soda water.

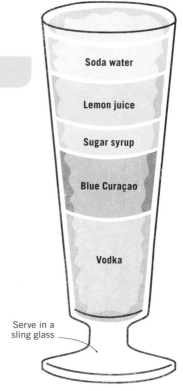

Soda water

Lemon juice

Sugar syrup

Blue Curaçao

Vodka

Serve in a sling glass

EXTRAS

GARNISH with a simple lemon wheel to add aroma and to create a striking colour contrast.

HURRICANE

Simplicity itself, but utterly delicious, this tropical cocktail was born in Pat O'Brien's bar in New Orleans in the 1940s. The Hurricane was created to use up a surplus of dark rum that the bar wanted to offload in order to buy whisky, which was more popular. Ironically, the drink was such a success, especially among sailors, that more rum had to be ordered to supply the demand for cocktails.

THE CLASSIC RECIPE

You can make the passion fruit syrup yourself (see p.31).

1. Place 50ml (1²/₃fl oz) Jamaican aged rum, 30ml (1fl oz) passion fruit syrup, 20ml (²/₃fl oz) lemon juice, and the pulp from ¹/₂ passion fruit in a blender.
2. Add crushed ice up to the top of the liquid and flash blend for no more than 5 seconds.
3. Pour into a hurricane glass.

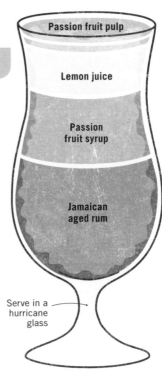

Passion fruit pulp

Lemon juice

Passion fruit syrup

Jamaican aged rum

Serve in a hurricane glass

EXTRAS

TOP with a 1/2 passion fruit, a lemon wheel, and a "windswept" umbrella turned inside out.

TURN OVER FOR REINVENTIONS ▶

HURRICANE REINVENTED

- 50ml (1²/₃fl oz) premium aged rum
- 2 dashes of Angostura bitters
- Pulp of ½ passion fruit
- 2 tsp brown sugar
- 3 clementine segments

TWISTER

In this classy variant, the fresh clementine and bitters give a sophisticated tang. In a shaker, muddle the clementine, the brown sugar, the passion fruit, and the Angostura bitters. Add the rum, fill the shaker with ice, and shake. Fine strain into a champagne flute.

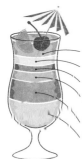

- 30ml (1fl oz) orange juice
- 15ml (½fl oz) lime juice
- 10ml (⅓fl oz) grenadine
- 15ml (½fl oz) passion fruit syrup
- 30ml (1fl oz) dark rum
- 30ml (1fl oz) white rum

HURRICANE NO. 2

You can make your own passion fruit syrup (see p.31) for this tangy, fruity twist. Combine all the ingredients in a shaker. Fill the shaker with ice and shake. Strain into a hurricane glass filled with crushed ice. Garnish with an orange wedge, a cherry, and a cocktail umbrella.

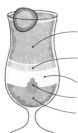

LOSE THE
BOOZE

- 60ml (2fl oz) orange juice
- Pulp of 1 passion fruit
- 15ml (½fl oz) lemon juice
- 1 tsp brown sugar
- 25ml (⁴/₅fl oz) passion fruit syrup

NEW ORLEANS BREEZE

A non-alcoholic twist. You can make your own passion fruit syrup (see p.31). Place all the ingredients in a blender. Fill with crushed ice up to the top of the liquid. Flash blend for no more than 5 seconds, then pour into a hurricane glass. Garnish with a passion fruit shell filled with a small scoop of passion fruit sorbet.

MOJITO

During the Prohibition era, many great American bartenders moved to work in Cuba. Familiar spirits such as bourbon weren't available, so they started substituting delicious, light-style Cuban rum in the classic recipes instead. The Mojito was probably invented at this time as a twist on the Mint Julep. The famous Cuban bar La Bodeguita claims it made the first Mojito.

THE CLASSIC RECIPE

The fresh-tasting combination of mint and lime gives the Mojito its distinctive character.

1. Place 8 mint leaves, 20ml (²/₃fl oz) sugar syrup, and 20ml (²/₃fl oz) lime juice in a highball glass. Press the mint leaves gently with the back of a spoon to release the flavour.

2. Add 50ml (1²/₃fl oz) white rum, fill the glass with crushed ice, and churn slowly for 5–10 seconds.

3. Add 20ml (²/₃fl oz) soda water and top with crushed ice.

Serve in a highball glass

Soda water

White rum

Lime juice

Mint leaves

Sugar syrup

EXTRAS

A GENEROUS mint sprig is all you need to garnish this classic.

TURN OVER FOR REINVENTIONS ▶

MOJITO REINVENTED

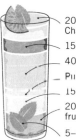

- 20ml (²/₃fl oz) Champagne
- 15ml (¹/₂fl oz) Aperol
- 40ml (1¹/₃fl oz) gin
- Pulp of ¹/₄ passion fruit
- 15ml (¹/₂fl oz) lime juice
- 20ml (²/₃fl oz) passion fruit syrup
- 5–6 mint leaves

ROYAL PALACE MOJITO

For passion fruit syrup see page 31.
Place the mint, passion fruit syrup, lime juice, and passion fruit pulp in a highball glass. Press the mint gently with the back of a spoon to release the flavour. Add the gin and Aperol, fill the glass with crushed ice, and churn slowly. Add the Champagne and top with crushed ice. Garnish with a mint sprig and ¹/₄ of a passion fruit.

- 40ml (1¹/₃fl oz) ginger ale
- 50ml (1³/₄fl oz) coconut rum liqueur
- 15ml (¹/₂fl oz) lime juice
- 10ml (¹/₃fl oz) sugar syrup
- 6 mint leaves

COCO MOJO

A tasty twist with a coconut flavour. Place the mint, sugar syrup, and lime juice in a highball glass. Press the mint gently with the back of a spoon to release the flavour. Add the coconut rum liqueur and fill the glass with crushed ice. Churn for 5–10 seconds. Add the ginger ale and top with crushed ice. Garnish with a mint sprig and slices of fresh ginger.

LOSE THE
BOOZE

- 40ml (1¹/₃fl oz) ginger beer
- 40ml (1¹/₃fl oz) pineapple juice
- 20ml (²/₃fl oz) lime juice
- 20ml (²/₃fl oz) mango syrup
- 8 mint leaves

MANGO MOJITO

A fruity mocktail twist on the classic.
Place the mint, mango syrup, and lime juice in a highball glass. Press the mint gently with the back of a spoon to release the flavour. Add the pineapple juice, fill the glass with crushed ice, and churn for 5–10 seconds. Add the ginger beer and top with crushed ice. Garnish with a mint sprig.

Nui NUI

"Nui" means "big" in Hawaiian and this cocktail is definitely big on flavour. The warming spices make it a great winter drink, as well as a tempting summer cocktail. This delicious classic was invented in 1937 by Don the Beachcomber, founder of the eponymous restaurant and bar which started the craze for tiki drinks in the early 1930s.

THE CLASSIC RECIPE

You can make the cinnamon syrup at home (see p.31).

1. Pour 50ml (1²/₃fl oz) aged rum, 5ml (¹/₆fl oz) vanilla liqueur, 5ml (¹/₆fl oz) Pimento Dram, 1 dash of Angostura bitters, 10ml (¹/₃fl oz) cinnamon syrup, 15ml (¹/₂fl oz) lime juice, and 20ml (²/₃fl oz) orange juice into a shaker.

2. Fill the shaker with crushed ice, then shake.

3. Pour into a rocks glass.

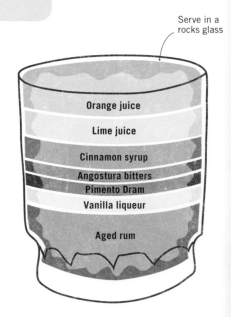

Serve in a rocks glass

Orange juice

Lime juice

Cinnamon syrup

Angostura bitters

Pimento Dram

Vanilla liqueur

Aged rum

LOSE THE BOOZE

For a non-alcoholic alternative, substitute fresh pineapple juice for the rum, liqueurs, and bitters.

EXTRAS

GARNISH WITH a simple orange twist or see page 38 to make the pictured orange feather.

Miami VICE

This is one of the most underrated cocktails – because it features two well-known classics, the Piña Colada and the Strawberry Daiquiri in the same glass, it isn't always taken seriously. Yet coconut and strawberry are a fantastic flavour combination, and the different layers make it visually stunning. When perfectly balanced, it is a delicious guilty pleasure.

THE CLASSIC RECIPE

You can drink the two layers separately or mix them together for a different taste.

1. To make the Strawberry Daiquiri, place 30ml (1fl oz) light white rum, 15ml (¹/₂fl oz) sugar syrup, 10ml (¹/₃fl oz) lime juice, and 3 strawberries in a blender.

2. Fill the blender with crushed ice up to the top of the liquid, then blend for 20–30 seconds. Pour into a large hurricane glass.

3. Next, make the Piña Colada by placing 30ml (1fl oz) Puerto Rican gold rum, 1 dash of Angostura bitters, 20ml (²/₃fl oz) fresh pineapple juice, and 15ml (¹/₂fl oz) coconut cream syrup (Reàl) in the blender.

4. Fill the blender with crushed ice up to the top of the liquid, then blend for 20–30 seconds.

5. Slowly pour the Piña Colada on top of the Strawberry Daiquiri.

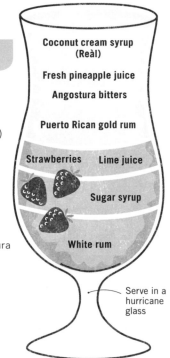

Coconut cream syrup (Reàl)

Fresh pineapple juice

Angostura bitters

Puerto Rican gold rum

Strawberries   Lime juice

Sugar syrup

White rum

Serve in a hurricane glass

EXTRAS

GARNISH with a pineapple wedge and a strawberry on a cocktail stick.

TURN OVER FOR REINVENTIONS ▶

MIAMI VICE REINVENTED

10ml (⅓fl oz) lime juice
10ml (⅓fl oz) sugar syrup
20ml (⅔fl oz) coconut rum liqueur
50ml (1⅔fl oz) white rum
2 strawberries
1 pineapple ring

SIN CITY

A spin on the Miami Vice that's shaken, not blended with ice. Muddle the pineapple and strawberries at the bottom of a shaker. Add the remaining ingredients, fill the shaker with ice, and shake hard. Strain into a chilled martini glass. Garnish with pineapple balls and a strawberry on a cocktail stick.

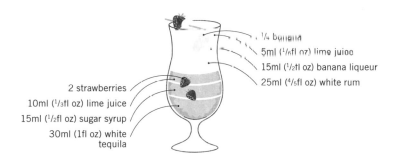

¼ banana
5ml (⅙fl oz) lime juice
15ml (½fl oz) banana liqueur
25ml (⅘fl oz) white rum

2 strawberries
10ml (⅓fl oz) lime juice
15ml (½fl oz) sugar syrup
30ml (1fl oz) white tequila

JALISCO CON CARIBE

This tropical variation combines a Strawberry Margarita with a Banana Daiquiri. Make the Strawberry Margarita by adding the tequila, sugar syrup, lime juice, and strawberries to a blender. Fill the blender with crushed ice up to the top of the liquid, then blend for 20–30 seconds. Pour into a large hurricane glass. Next, make the Banana Daiquiri by adding the white rum, banana liqueur, lime juice, and ¼ banana to the blender. Fill the blender with crushed ice up to the top of the liquid, then blend for 20–30 seconds. Slowly pour the mixture on top of the Strawberry Margarita. Garnish with a banana ball and a strawberry on a cocktail stick.

Sex on the BEACH

Now one of the most popular cocktails in the world, there are a few theories about how the recipe was invented. One story is that a bartender called Ted from Confetti's Bar in Florida created the drink in the 1980s to win a bonus offered by a peach schnapps company. He allegedly named the drink Sex on the Beach after the two main attractions that lured visitors to Florida during spring break.

THE CLASSIC RECIPE

Simple to make, summery, and sweet-tasting.

1. Pour 50ml (1²/₃fl oz) vodka, 25ml (⁴/₅fl oz) peach liqueur, 35ml (1¹/₅fl oz) cranberry juice, and 35ml (1¹/₅fl oz) orange juice into a shaker.
2. Fill the shaker with ice, shake, then strain into a highball glass filled with ice cubes.

Serve in a highball glass

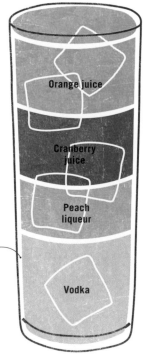

Orange juice

Cranberry juice

Peach liqueur

Vodka

LOSE THE
BOOZE

Replace the vodka and peach liqueur with peach syrup and extra cranberry juice and orange juice.

EXTRAS

AN ORANGE slice, twisted around a glacé cherry and held together by a cocktail stick, makes the perfect garnish.

TURN OVER FOR REINVENTIONS ▶

SEX ON THE BEACH REINVENTED

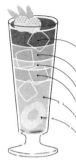

- 25ml (⁴/₅fl oz) cranberry juice
- 25ml (⁴/₅fl oz) orange juice
- 10ml (¹/₃fl oz) lychee liqueur
- 15ml (¹/₂fl oz) peach liqueur
- 50ml (1²/₃fl oz) vodka
- 1 fresh pineapple ring

SANDY BOTTOMS

The lychee liqueur and pineapple add extra tropical flavours. Muddle the pineapple ring in the bottom of a shaker. Add the remaining ingredients, fill the shaker with ice, and shake hard. Strain into a sling glass filled with ice cubes. Garnish with 3 pineapple leaves and 2 lychees covered with brown sugar.

- 100ml (3¹/₂fl oz) Champagne
- 15ml (¹/₂fl oz) orange juice
- 10ml (¹/₃fl oz) grenadine
- 10ml (¹/₃fl oz) peach liqueur
- 25ml (⁴/₅fl oz) vodka

ROYAL SEX ON THE BEACH

A bubbly variant on the classic. Combine all the ingredients except the Champagne in a shaker. Fill the shaker with ice, shake, then fine strain into a chilled Champagne flute. Top with Champagne (or any other sparkling wine) and garnish with a single edible flower.

- 15ml (¹/₂fl oz) crème de mûre
- 20ml (²/₃fl oz) pineapple juice
- 15ml (¹/₂fl oz) lime juice
- 10ml (¹/₃fl oz) Cointreau Blood Orange
- 15ml (¹/₂fl oz) peach liqueur
- 40ml (1¹/₃fl oz) gin

RED ANKLES

A cheeky twist on Sex on the Beach with a gin base. Combine all the ingredients except the crème de mûre in a shaker. Fill the shaker with ice, shake, then strain into a poco grande glass filled with crushed ice. Float the crème de mûre on top. Garnish with 2 blackberries.

Rum RUNNER

This cocktail was created in the late 1950s by the Holiday Isle Resort Tiki bar on Islamorada in the Florida Keys to use up an excess of rum. The name refers to the "rum runners" who smuggled alcohol from the Caribbean to America during the Prohibition era via the Keys. With international waters lying only 3 kilometres away, there was plenty of opportunity for selling and drinking rum.

THE CLASSIC RECIPE

You can use aged rum instead of dark rum if you prefer.

1. Pour 30ml (1fl oz) gold rum, 30ml (1fl oz) dark rum, 1 dash of Angostura bitters, 20ml (²/₃fl oz) crème de mûre, 20ml (²/₃fl oz) crème de bananes, 5ml (¹/₆fl oz) grenadine, 20ml (²/₃fl oz) lime juice, 30ml (1fl oz) pineapple juice, and 30ml (1fl oz) orange juice into a shaker.

2. Fill the shaker with ice, shake, and strain into a rocks glass filled with ice cubes.

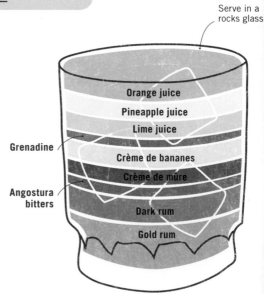

Serve in a rocks glass

Orange juice

Pineapple juice

Lime juice

Grenadine

Crème de bananes

Crème de mûre

Angostura bitters

Dark rum

Gold rum

EXTRAS

GARNISH with a pineapple wedge, an orange twist, and a blackberry skewered on a cocktail stick.

Innovative recipes straight from **Georgi's** imagination, with the occasional exciting contribution from **award-winning** guest bartenders. These **irresistible cocktails** are the perfect blend of tropical **tradition** and **contemporary mixology.** Your only problem will be choosing which one to start with!

MODERN
TROPICAL COCKTAILS

Taki FUGU

Takifugu is a delicacy in Japan; a type of pufferfish, it can be poisonous if not prepared correctly. Far from poisonous, this perfectly balanced cocktail uses bean sprouts and sake in a fun homage to Japanese dining. Many tiki bars also use pufferfish as decoration – the perfect meshing of drinking and culture.

THE MODERN RECIPE

The unusual, earthy flavour of the muddled bean sprouts is balanced by the refreshing cucumber.

1. Muddle a thin slice of cucumber, 6 bean sprouts, and 3 tsp caster sugar at the bottom of a shaker.
2. Add 40ml (1¹/₃fl oz) white rum, 20ml (²/₃fl oz) honjozo sake, 15ml (¹/₂fl oz) lime juice, 10ml (¹/₃fl oz) lemon juice, 5ml (¹/₆fl oz) white balsamic vinegar, and 20ml (²/₃fl oz) pink grapefruit juice.
3. Fill the shaker with ice, and shake hard, then strain into a brandy balloon filled with ice cubes.
4. Top with 30ml (1fl oz) ginger beer.

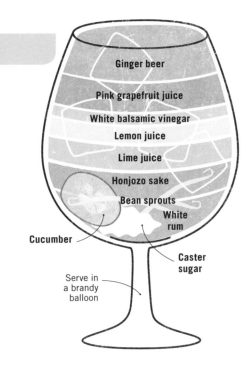

Ginger beer

Pink grapefruit juice

White balsamic vinegar

Lemon juice

Lime juice

Honjozo sake

Bean sprouts

White rum

Cucumber

Caster sugar

Serve in a brandy balloon

LOSE THE
BOOZE

For a non-alcoholic variation replace all of the alcohol with green tea.

EXTRAS

CREATE A striking garnish by cutting a large cucumber slice and balancing a few bean sprouts on top.

Tiki DADDY G

Proving that tropical drinks don't always need to evoke summer, this tiki-style cocktail is like Christmas in a glass. Spicy yet refreshing, the rum base brings flavours of cinnamon, dark chocolate, and Angostura bitters. The Tiki Daddy G is the perfect cocktail for a Halloween or Christmas celebration.

THE MODERN RECIPE

You can use any pumpkin-spiced syrup in place of Reàl, but the consistency may differ.

1. Pour 50ml (1²/₃fl oz) Amaro di Angostura, 20ml (²/₃fl oz) Pumpkin syrup (Reàl), 20ml (²/₃fl oz) lime juice, 25ml (⁴/₅fl oz) apple juice, and 25ml (⁴/₅fl oz) orange juice into a shaker.
2. Fill the shaker with ice and shake.
3. Strain into a highball tiki glass filled with crushed ice.

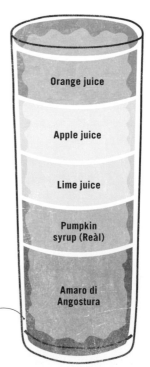

Orange juice

Apple juice

Lime juice

Pumpkin syrup (Reàl)

Amaro di Angostura

Serve in a highball tiki glass

LOSE THE
BOOZE

For a non-alcoholic variation, take away all of the alcohol and replace with green tea.

EXTRAS

GARNISH with an orange wheel and apple slices, skewered on a cinnamon stick. Burn the cinnamon for extra aroma.

Beach WHACKER

This slips down easily but is deceptively strong and boozy! The Christmassy flavours of cinnamon, cloves, and vanilla from the spiced maple syrup, and almond notes from the orgeat, marry beautifully with the classic, tropical taste of lime and grapefruit.

THE MODERN RECIPE

You can make spiced maple syrup at home (see p.31).

1. Muddle a pineapple ring in a shaker.
2. Add 40ml (1¹⁄₃fl oz) gold rum, 20ml (²⁄₃fl oz) apricot brandy, 20ml (²⁄₃fl oz) vanilla liqueur, 10ml (¹⁄₃fl oz) orgeat syrup, 10ml (¹⁄₃fl oz) spiced maple syrup, and 25ml (⁴⁄₅fl oz) lime juice to the shaker.
3. Fill the shaker with ice, shake hard, then strain into a sling glass filled with ice cubes.
4. Top with 20ml (²⁄₃fl oz) grapefruit soda water.

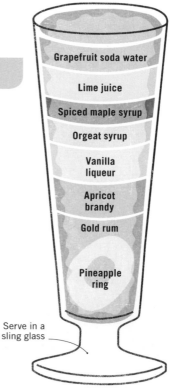

Grapefruit soda water

Lime juice

Spiced maple syrup

Orgeat syrup

Vanilla liqueur

Apricot brandy

Gold rum

Pineapple ring

Serve in a sling glass

LOSE THE BOOZE

Earl Grey tea makes a great booze replacement in this cocktail.

EXTRAS

DUST THE TOP with ground cinnamon and garnish with a pineapple leaf and a pineapple wedge.

Tropical APPLE TOFFEE

The use of spices such as cinnamon, nutmeg, and cloves is very common in tiki cocktails, but traditionally they are paired with flavours of pineapple and orange. In this modern nod to the tiki classics, toffee, apple juice, and passion fruit are used to perfectly balance the exotic, spicy rum base.

THE MODERN RECIPE

You can make your own falernum at home (see p.33).

1. Place 50ml (1²/₃fl oz) spiced rum, 1 dash of Angostura bitters, 20ml (²/₃fl oz) falernum, 20ml (²/₃fl oz) toffee syrup, 50ml (1²/₃fl oz) apple juice, and the pulp from ¹/₂ passion fruit into a shaker.
2. Fill the shaker with ice, shake, then strain into a rocks glass filled with ice cubes.

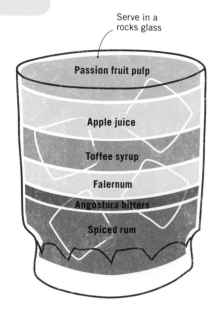

Serve in a rocks glass

Passion fruit pulp

Apple juice

Toffee syrup

Falernum

Angostura bitters

Spiced rum

EXTRAS

GARNISH with an apple fan, and a hard toffee sweet in a passion fruit shell.

Tiki Tiki BANG BANG

With its rum base, spice notes, juices, and syrups, this is a modern take on a classic tiki-style drink. Watch out – it is packed with flavour, but in true tiki-style, it's also incredibly strong; if you're not careful, you could be banging your head! Like all tiki drinks it calls for some theatrical presentation – garnish generously!

THE MODERN RECIPE

You can make the cinnamon syrup yourself (see p.31).

1. Pour 40ml (1¹/₃fl oz) gold rum, 20ml (²/₃fl oz) dark rum, 2 dashes of Angostura bitters, 20ml (²/₃fl oz) mango syrup, 15ml (¹/₂fl oz) cinnamon syrup, 5ml (¹/₆fl oz) natural agave nectar, 30ml (1fl oz) lime juice, 30ml (1fl oz) orange juice, and 30ml (1fl oz) pineapple juice into a shaker.
2. Fill the shaker with ice, shake, and strain into a highball glass filled with crushed ice.

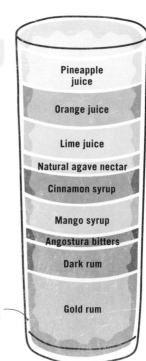

Pineapple juice

Orange juice

Lime juice

Natural agave nectar

Cinnamon syrup

Mango syrup

Angostura bitters

Dark rum

Serve in a highball glass

Gold rum

LOSE THE
BOOZE

Substitute extra orange juice and pineapple juice for the rum, to turn this boozy drink into a mocktail.

EXTRAS

GARNISH with a slice of mango, and an orange twist wrapped around a pineapple wedge.

Laki LAMBO

Powerful and elegant – like a Lamborghini – this cocktail will definitely make you feel lucky. The pineapple foam and caramelized coconut sugar that tops this classical-style cocktail gives it a fun tropical twist (a nod to the Piña Colada). The rum, Cognac, and Cointreau provide a rich dark base, cut through by the citrus of the lemon juice.

THE MODERN RECIPE

Honey water is easy to make at home (see p.30).

1. Place 25ml (⁴/₅fl oz) aged agricole rum, 25ml (⁴/₅fl oz) VSOP Cognac, 15ml (¹/₂fl oz) Cointreau Blood Orange, 15ml (¹/₂fl oz) honey water, and 15ml (¹/₂fl oz) lemon juice in a shaker.
2. Fill the shaker with ice and shake hard, then strain into a chilled martini glass.
3. Whisk 50ml (1²/₃fl oz) pineapple juice with ½ egg white until very frothy.
4. Pour the froth on top of the cocktail, keeping back any liquid.
5. Sprinkle the top with coconut sugar. You can caramelize this with a blowtorch if you have one.

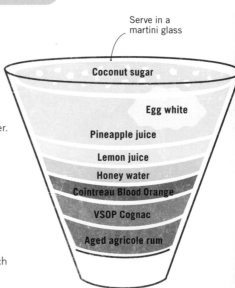

Serve in a martini glass

Coconut sugar

Egg white

Pineapple juice

Lemon juice

Honey water

Cointreau Blood Orange

VSOP Cognac

Aged agricole rum

EXTRAS

A DELICATE edible flower makes a simple, sophisticated garnish.

Golden SAND

Named after a famous beach on the Black Sea in northern Bulgaria, this cocktail captures the essence of summer – sun, sea, and beautiful golden sand. A modern take on classic tiki combinations, the tropical notes of rum, banana, and fresh orange work to perfectly balance the anise flavour of the absinthe.

THE MODERN RECIPE

The egg yolk creates a thick, velvety consistency and beautiful colour.

1. Whisk 1 egg yolk with 2 tsp caster sugar until the sugar has dissolved and the mixture is frothy.
2. Add 40ml (1¹/₃fl oz) aged rum, 10ml (¹/₃fl oz) absinthe, 20ml (²/₃fl oz) banana liqueur, 20ml (²/₃fl oz) lime juice, and 30ml (1fl oz) orange juice.
3. Fill the shaker with ice and shake hard.
4. Fine strain into a rocks glass filled with ice cubes.

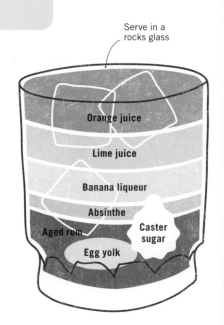

Serve in a rocks glass

Orange juice

Lime juice

Banana liqueur

Absinthe

Aged rum

Caster sugar

Egg yolk

EXTRAS

SPRINKLE a little grated nutmeg on top and garnish with a big orange twist.

English TEA-KI GARDEN

Developed by Ian Burrell, global rum ambassador and founder of the UK Rum Festival, this superb cocktail brings together the best of English ingredients. With tea, rhubarb, gin, and raspberries, it's the perfect tipple for a summer garden party.

THE MODERN RECIPE

You can use raspberry liqueur instead of syrup. Try making your own raspberry syrup at home (see p.31).

1. Place 50ml (1²/₃fl oz) Barbados gold rum, 10ml (¹/₃fl oz) rhubarb gin, 10ml (¹/₃fl oz) raspberry syrup, 15ml (¹/₂fl oz) rhubarb purée, 10ml (¹/₃fl oz) lemon juice, 20ml (²/₃fl oz) cold black tea, and 10ml (¹/₃fl oz) cloudy apple juice in a shaker.
2. Fill the shaker with ice, shake, then strain into a highball glass filled with ice cubes.

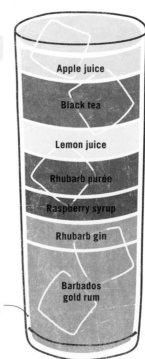

Apple juice

Black tea

Lemon juice

Rhubarb purée

Raspberry syrup

Rhubarb gin

Barbados gold rum

Serve in a highball glass

LOSE THE
BOOZE

For a non-alcoholic variation, substitute extra tea and rhubarb syrup for the rum and gin.

EXTRAS

GARNISH with fresh rhubarb sticks, raspberries, and an apple fan (see p.38).

MAKANA

This tiki-style cocktail is the perfect marriage of spices and sweetness. It was created by Daniele Dalla Pola, owner of the Nu Lounge bar in Bologna, Italy, and creator of the Sexy Colada – a twist on the Piña Colada. Makana means "gift" in Hawaiian, and this is the perfect way to spoil your friends.

THE MODERN RECIPE

Mango syrup provides the essential tropical flavour here – see page 31 to make it.

1. Place 45ml (1½fl oz) gold rum, 15ml (½fl oz) bourbon, 2 dashes of Angostura bitters, 30ml (1fl oz) mango syrup, 2 dashes of vanilla extract, and 30ml (1fl oz) lime juice in a blender.

2. Add crushed ice up to the top of the liquid and flash blend for no more than 5 seconds.

3. Pour into a tiki glass or highball glass and top with 50ml (1²⁄₃fl oz) ginger beer.

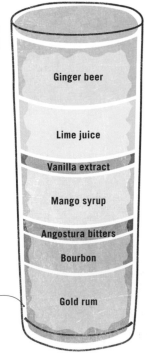

Ginger beer

Lime juice

Vanilla extract

Mango syrup

Angostura bitters

Bourbon

Serve in a tiki glass or highball glass

Gold rum

EXTRAS

ADD A SIMPLE garnish of 2 generous mint sprigs.

Lanai PUNCH

"Lanai" means a patio or veranda in Hawaiian, and this is the perfect drink to complete a romantic moment on your patio overlooking the ocean. Delicate rose petals complement the flavours of the black cherry syrup and the guava juice. A very unusual, but utterly delicious, combination of flavours for a tropical cocktail.

THE MODERN RECIPE

You can use cherry liqueur instead of black cherry syrup if you prefer.

1. Place 60ml (2fl oz) premium aged rum, 20ml (²/₃fl oz) black cherry syrup (Reàl), 10ml (¹/₃fl oz) rose syrup, 25ml (⁴/₅fl oz) lemon juice, and 40ml (1¹/₃fl oz) guava juice in a shaker.

2. Fill the shaker with ice, shake, then strain into a rocks glass filled with ice cubes.

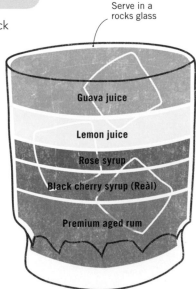

Serve in a rocks glass

Guava juice

Lemon juice

Rose syrup

Black cherry syrup (Reàl)

Premium aged rum

LOSE THE BOOZE

It's easy to turn this cocktail into a delicious mocktail – simply swap the rum for any red bush tea.

EXTRAS

FOR A SPECIAL GARNISH, top with rose petals and turkish delight in a crushed ice cup (see p.38). Complete with a dusting of icing sugar.

Wiki TIKI

This wicked tiki cocktail – the Wiki Tiki – is a standout combination of flavours. It's rare to find a tiki drink made with vodka, but this modern take on the classic style really hits the mark. With refreshing watermelon and mint, and delicate elderflower, it evokes the essence of summer.

THE MODERN RECIPE

A delicious long drink for a hot summer's evening.

1. Muddle 4 mint leaves and 2 slices of watermelon in a shaker.
2. Add 50ml (1²/₃fl oz) vodka, 15ml (¹/₂fl oz) elderflower cordial, 10ml (¹/₃fl oz) grenadine, and 20ml (²/₃fl oz) cranberry juice.
3. Fill the shaker with ice and shake hard.
4. Fine strain into a sling glass filled with ice cubes, then top with crushed ice.

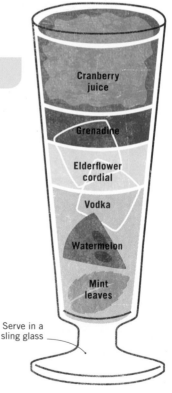

Cranberry juice

Grenadine

Elderflower cordial

Vodka

Watermelon

Mint leaves

Serve in a sling glass

LOSE THE
BOOZE

Swap the vodka
for extra watermelon
for a refreshing,
booze-free
variation.

EXTRAS

BE BOLD with this
garnish. A large
slice of watermelon
makes a striking
drink topper. Mint
also works well.

Angels' SHARE

Drinks for sharing need to be crowd-pleasers with flavours that satisfy all tastes. Here, white rum, pineapple, and orange juice bring the tropical notes, with elderflower and apricot adding aroma. Mint adds freshness, working as a buffer for all the flavours. The Prosecco bubbles make it elegant and delicious. See pages 40–41 to turn other drinks in this book into sharing cocktails.

THE MODERN RECIPE

Make your own honey water at home (see p.30).

1. Pour 380ml (12³/₄fl oz) white rum, 180ml (6fl oz) apricot brandy, 70ml (2¹/₃fl oz) St. Germain elderflower liqueur, 130ml (4¹/₃fl oz) honey water, 250ml (9fl oz) pineapple juice, 250ml (9fl oz) orange juice, and 50 mint leaves into a big punch bowl filled with ice cubes.

2. Pour in 1 bottle of Prosecco.

3. Swizzle to marry the ingredients together.

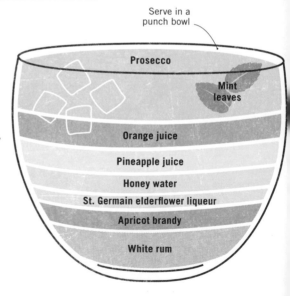

Serve in a punch bowl

Prosecco

Mint leaves

Orange juice

Pineapple juice

Honey water

St. Germain elderflower liqueur

Apricot brandy

White rum

EXTRAS

GARNISH with a mixture of fruits, mint sprigs, and flowers. Serve with long straws.

INDEX

A

almonds: falernum 33
Amaro di Angostura:
  Tiki Daddy G 120–21
Angels' Share 140–41
apple juice:
  London Fog Cutter 79
  Tiki Daddy G 120–21
  Tropical Apple Toffee 124–25
apricot brandy:
  Angels' Share 140–41

B

banana liqueur:
  Golden Sand 130–31
bananas: Banana Daiquiri 55
Beach Whacker 122–23
black cherry syrup:
  Lanai Punch 136–37
Blue Curaçao:
  Blue Hawaii 70–71
  Blue Lagoon 94–95

C

Cachaça 17:
  Caipirinha 46–47
  Tropicaipirinha 49
Campari: Jungle Bird 80–81
Capirinella 49
Champagne: Royal Palace
  Mojito 103
  Royal Sex on the Beach 113
cinnamon syrup 31
cocktails: equipment 18–21
  glassware 22–24
  history 8–11
  making your own mixes 34–35
  mixing and shaking 26–29
  sharing 40–41
Coco Kane 63
Coco Mojo 103
coconut cream syrup 32
  Coco Kane 63
  Piña Colada 60–61
  Sexy Colada 63
  Virgin Colada 63
coconut water:
  Piña Caipirinha 49
  Rum Punch 56–57
  Virgin Colada 63

Cognac: Finest Cut 79
  Fog Cutter 76–77
  Laki Lambo 128–29
Cointreau: Margarita 82–83
  Singapore Slang 69
  Singapore Sling 66–67
  Tequila on the Beach 85
cranberry juice: Sandy
  Bottoms 113
  Sex on the Beach 110–11
  Wiki Tiki 138–39
Curaçao 17

DE

Daiquiri 42, 52–53
  Banana Daiquiri 55
  Hemingway Daiquiri 55
  South Seas Daiquiri 55
Disco Mai Tai 75
Earl Grey tea: Grog o'Clock 59
English Tea-Ki Garden 132–33
equipment 18–21, 41

F

falernum 33
  South Seas Daiquiri 55
  Tropical Apple Toffee 124–25
Finest Cut 79
Fog Cutter 76–77
fruit: fruit syrups 31
  garnishes 37, 39
  hollowed fruits 25

G

gardenia mix 32
  Jewel of the Sea 93
  Pearl Diver 90
garnishes 36–39
gin: Capirinella 49
  London Fog Cutter 79
  Murky Morning 79
  Red Ankles 113
  Royal Palace Mojito 103
  Singapore Slang 69
  Singapore Sling 66–67
  Tiki Sing Sling 69
ginger ale: Coco Mojo 103
  Scottish Sling 69
ginger beer: Mango Mojito 103
  Taki Fugu 118–19
ginger syrup 31
glassware 22–24
Golden Sand 130–31

grapefruit juice: Pink Merry 85
Grog o'Clock 59
guava juice: Lanai Punch 136–37

H

Hemingway Daiquiri 55
history 8–11
honey cream 32
honey water 30
Honolulu Honey 93
Hurricane 43, 96–97
Hurricane No.2 99

IJ

ice bowl, crushed 38
Innocent Mai Tai 75
Jalisco Con Caribe 109
Jamaican Punch 41, 59
Jewel of the Sea 93
Jungle Bird 43, 80–81

L

Laki Lambo 128–29
Lanai Punch 136–37
lemon juice: Blue Lagoon 94–95
  Lanai Punch 136–37
  Tiki Sing Sling 69
lime juice: Beach Whacker
  122–23
  Daiquiri 52–53
  Mai Thai 75
  Makana 134–35
  Margarita 82–83
  Mojito 100–101
  Queen's Park Swizzle 50–51
  Tiki Tiki Bang Bang 126–27
London Fog Cutter 79

MN

Mai Tai 72–73
Mai Thai 75
Makana 134–35
mandarin juice: Murky
  Morning 79
mango purée: Honolulu
  Honey 93
mango syrup: Makana 134–35
  Mango Mojito 103
  Tropicaipirinha 49
maple syrup, spiced 31
Margarita 9, 43, 82–83
Martini, Pornstar 64–65
mezcal 17

Oaxaca Sunrise 89
Miami Vice 106–107
mixing cocktails 28–29
Mojitos 100–101
  Royal Palace Mojito 41, 103
Murky Morning 79
New Orleans Breeze 99
Nui Nui 104–105

O

Oaxaca Sunrise 89
orange Curaçao: Mai Tai 72–73
orange juice: Angels' Share
  140–41
  Coco Kane 63
  Finest Cut 79
  Fog Cutter 76–77
  Golden Sand 130–31
  Hurricane No.2 99
  Innocent Mai Tai 75
  Jamaican punch 59
  New Orleans Breeze 99
  Oaxaca Sunrise 89
  Rum Runner 114–15
  Sandy Bottoms 113
  Sex on the Beach 110–11
  Tequila Sunrise 86–87
  Tequila Sunset 89
  Tiki Tiki Bang Bang 126–27
Orchidea 41, 85

PQ

passion fruit: Pornstar Martini
  64–65
passion fruit syrup:
  Hurricane 96–97
  New Orleans Breeze 99
  Royal Palace Mojito 103
peach liqueur: Sex on the
  Beach 110–11
Pearl Diver 90
Piña Caipirinha 49
Piña Colada 60–61
pineapple juice:
  Angels' Share 140–41
  Honolulu Honey 93
  Innocent Mai Tai 75
  Jamaican Punch 59
  Jungle Bird 80–81
  Mango Mojito 103
  Piña Caipirinha 49
  Piña Colada 60–61
  Rum Runner 114–15
  Sexy Colada 63

Tiki Tiki Bang Bang 126–27
Virgin Colada 63
Pink Merry 85
Pisco 17
Pornstar Martini 64–65
pumpkin syrup:
  Tiki Daddy G 120–21
Queen's Park Swizzle 42, 50–51

R

Red Ankles 113
Royal Palace Mojito 41, 103
Royal Sex on the Beach 113
rum 8–10, 12–15
  Angels' Share 140–41
  Banana Daiquiri 55
  Beach Whacker 122–23
  Blue Hawaii 70–71
  Coco Kane 63
  Coco Mojo 103
  Daiquiri 52–53
  Disco Mai Tai 75
  English Tea-Ki Garden 132–33
  falernum 33
  Finest Cut 79
  Fog Cutter 76–77
  Golden Sand 130–31
  Grog o'Clock 59
  Hemingway Daiquiri 55
  Honolulu Honey 93
  Hurricane 96–97
  Hurricane No.2 99
  Jalisco Con Caribe 109
  Jamaican punch 59
  Jewel of the Sea 93
  Jungle Bird 80–81
  Laki Lambo 128–29
  Lanai Punch 136–37
  Mai Tai 72–73
  Mai Thai 75
  Makana 134–35
  Miami Vice 106–107
  Mojito 100–101
  Murky Morning 79
  Nui Nui 104–105
  Pearl Diver 90
  Piña Colada 60–61
  Queen's Park Swizzle 50–51
  Rum Punches 42, 56–57
  Rum Runner 41, 114–15
  Sexy Colada 63
  Sin City 109
  South Seas Daiquiri 55
  Taki Fugu 118–19

Tiki Sing Sling 69
Tiki Tiki Bang Bang 126–27
Tropical Apple Toffee 124–25
Twister 99

S

Sandy Bottoms 113
Scottish Sling 69
Sex on the Beach 43, 110–11
Sexy Colada 63
shaking cocktails 26–27
sharing cocktails 40–41
Sin City 109
Singapore Slang 69
Singapore Sling 66–67
South Seas Daiquiri 55
spices 35
  garnishes 37
  spiced syrups 31
syrups: coconut cream 32
  fruit 31
  spiced 31
  sugar 30

T

Taki Fugu 118–19
tequila 9, 16, 17
  Jalisco Con Caribe 109
  Margarita 82–83
  Orchidea 85
  Pink Merry 85
  Tequila on the Beach 85
  Tequila Sunrise 43, 86–87
  Tequila Sunset 89
Thai syrup 31
Tiki Daddy G 120–21
Tiki Sing Sling 69
Tiki Tiki Bang Bang 126–27
toffee syrup: Tropical Apple
  Toffee 124–25
Tropicaipirinha 42, 49
Tropical Apple Toffee 124–25
Twister 99

VW

Virgin Colada 63
vodka: Blue Lagoon 94–95
  Pornstar Martini 64–65
  Royal Sex on the Beach 113
  Sandy Bottoms 113
  Sex on the Beach 110–11
  Wiki Tiki 138–39
Wiki Tiki 43, 138–39

ABOUT THE AUTHOR

Georgi Radev is an award-winning global bartender with a love for all things tropical. He managed one of the most famous bars in London, Mahiki, for over a decade; has travelled all over the world to learn and teach about rum, tiki, and cocktails; and is the creator of the unique British festival, Spirit of Tiki. His latest venture is a brand-new London bar and authentic "tropical escape", Laki Kane. Unique in its approach, Laki Kane is the first bar in the world not to use refined sugar in any cocktails, and the first bar to have an on site micro rum distillery. It prides itself on providing a truly tropical experience, with the decor inspired by all major tropical regions and the drinks flavoured with traditional tropical ingredients.

ACKNOWLEDGMENTS

Georgi Radev would like to thank: My business partners, Steve Kyprianou and Sam Robson, for believing in my dream and always for being there for me. My wife, Radostina Radeva, for giving me the love, strength, and unconditional support to keep doing what I love. Douglas Ankrah, Richard Wood, Papa Jules, Ian Burrell, and Bill Hinkebein for helping me grow in my career and introducing me to all things tropical and rum. A big thank you to Jeff "Beachbum" Berry for dedicating his life to tiki and tiki cocktails and helping us better understand the magic of tropical drinks. Douglas Ankrah, Ian Burrell, and Daniele Dalla Pola for contributing cocktails to the book. DK and especially Laura Bithell for the opportunity to write this book, and for the professional support during the process. Most of all I want to thank all the bartenders around the world who are creating great cocktails and working so hard every night giving their heart and soul so you can have fun and be happy!

DK WOULD LIKE TO THANK:

Art direction and prop styling: Isabel de Cordova
Image retouching: Jörn Kröger
Proofreading: Anna Cheifetz and Poppy Blakiston Houston
Indexing: Vanessa Bird